GOD'S COVENANT

WITH YOU AND FOR YOU

NIYI OLUJOBI

CONTENTS

DEDICATION

Blessed be the God of Abraham, Isaac and Jacob who demonstrates His love and mercy to us all through covenants. This little book of mine, I send to all peoples, tribes, and nations across the world for revelation, instruction, and to whet the appetite of those who would go into deeper study of God's covenant.

Thanks be to God and Father of my Lord and Savior Jesus Christ who led saints before me to put their revelation on the topic of covenant in book form. Notable among them are E W Kenyon and Kenneth Copeland. I am blessed that I can start my study from their materials.

I am grateful to my church family (Church of His Presence, UK) – beautiful people to whom we do life together. You all have been encouragers and much needed family. I make special recognition of my friends who encouraged me to put these thoughts and knowing of mine into a book; and finally, my wife and children whom the God of covenant has given me. God bless you and much love from my heart to you all.

FORWARD

It's such a great pleasure to write the foreword for this treasured book: GOD'S COVENANT WITH YOU AND FOR YOU.

Covenant is an agreement of consolidated promise made between two people over an issue. The old covenant is based on animal's blood to typify the new and better covenant which is premise on the pure, holy, and unspotted blood of the lamb [Jesus Christ the first begotten of the dead] that cleanses once and for all. Unlike the old covenant that atonement needed to be made every now and then before sacrifices could be offered to God. A covenant is also a defined agreement usually backed by an oath to bind the two parties.

This book has been written to expose, educate and to reveal God's covenant with you and for you as citizen of God's kingdom. Let every believer, preacher, pastor, prophets, and parents read this book as the Holy spirit interprets God's plan and purpose of His covenant for His people.

In this book, as you read through you will see what covenant is all about, types of covenant, the power of God that keeps covenant, covenant case studies and how to have assurance of God's covenant in your life, family and ministry.

The author, Pastor Niyi is not just a preacher but a teacher of the word with deeper understanding of divine revelation of God's word, He is an addicted worshipper, a man of prayer, a giver and one who loves God in total obedience to his call.

I recommend this book for every life that wants to know more about covenant and its power.

Evangelist Mrs. Toun Soetan

Pastor Niyi Olujobi is a dear friend of mine. He is a man of deep humility, hunger for God and man of Prayer, Intimacy with God and Faith and one of the few men of God I know that truly has a revelation of what covenant is, because he is a man of covenant.

I am so glad he has put this revelation that he has been ministering on for many years into book form, because in the day and age we are in has the body of Christ as well has in our society and culture, because it most cultures specifically western culture has no or little understanding of Covenant. That's why I am so glad my good friend has put this revelation down in book form because we need to get a revelation and correct biblical understanding on covenant.

Many are saying we don't read the Old Covenant of the Word of God because we are New Covenant believers, which is true we are New Covenant Believers but there is so much we are missing out of from that phrase 'that Old Covenant is not relevant for us today'. In this book by my dear friend, you will get a biblical revelation of God's Covenant with you and for you! You will get a revelation that He truly is a Covenant keeping God.

I highly recommend this book it will transform your revelation of God the Father and His Covenant with you and for you.

Paul Dewar

Reachout Power Ministries

I have always had a keen interest in the subject of covenant, and I have been blessed by listening to teachings about covenant and speaking about it over the years.

So, when Pastor Niyi told me about publishing (GOD'S COVENANT WITH YOU AND FOR YOU) I was super intrigued.

Every day I see Christians enthusiastically professing their faith and love for God, but what is missing is a deep understanding that covenant is the bedrock upon which our relationship with God is built and anchored. Upon it we thrive and do great things for God.

Pastor Niyi's book shows how our knowledge of covenant from scriptural standpoints can support us in running our Christian race and fulfilling our destiny purpose with boldness and assurance instead of doubts and hesitations.

Well done Pastor Niyi for the amount of efforts, thoughtfulness, spiritual insight you put into this work. This book has depth. Thank you for being a blessing to us in the body of Christ.

Pastor Lanre Joda

RCCG Praise City, London

INTRODUCTION

Many of us view life from the lens of our upbringing, society, and education. Many of us understand the Bible (the word of God) from the perspective of our upbringing, society, and education. The point is we read and understand from the dominant mindset in our lives and that includes the bible. Hebrew thinking and Greek thinking are not the same, yet it is the Greek thinking that influences today's society and impacts many of our English translations of the Bible which was written by Hebrew thinkers.

As I studied the Bible recently, I realized that for most of my Christian life, I had understood the Bible from a Greek mindset and had very little understanding of covenants. Although, the concept of covenant is as old as the world itself, we must understand the Bible as a book of covenants from the Hebraic perspective to fully appropriate what the Lord has cut for us in His covenants.

Paul in his writing to the Romans said:

"And do not be conformed to this world, but be transformed by the renewing of your mind, that you may prove what is that good and acceptable and perfect will of God." (**Romans 12:2**)

I am using this verse of scripture to remind you that you are to allow the covenants of God to shape your thinking, your actions, your prayer, and your confidence. We must be committed to the process of transforming our minds and read scriptures from the perspective of a transformed mind.

Jesus came to the earth to establish the God covenant with man to which He (Jesus) is the Mediator. Jesus said to His disciples as He was rounding up His ministry on earth and fulfilling the purpose for which He was sent: *"for this is My blood of the new covenant, which is shed for many for the remission of sins." (Matthew 26:28)*. There is a new blood covenant that He was establishing by the shedding of His blood which is for many things, including the remission of sins.

What the blood of bulls, goats, birds, or other animals could not establish, the blood of Jesus did and that established the New Covenant. Hebrews 9:11-14 says:

"But Christ came as High Priest of the good things to come, with the greater and more perfect tabernacle not made with hands, that is, not of this creation. Not with the blood of goats and calves, but with His own blood He entered the Most Holy Place once for all, having obtained eternal redemption. For if the blood of bulls and goats and the ashes of a heifer, sprinkling the unclean, sanctifies for the purifying of the flesh, how much more shall the blood of Christ, who through the eternal Spirit offered Himself without spot to God, cleanse your conscience from dead works to serve the living God?"

The Bible states that our present covenant is better than the old covenant and it is established on better promises. What is this new covenant that you have with God? What are the terms of this covenant? What promises and/or blessings are attached to this covenant? What is your role in this covenant? How is this new covenant related to covenants cut with Abraham, Moses, David, etc.? Why would God cut covenant with man in the first place?

These answers and many more are contained in this book. I will encourage you to be patient and read to the end and I believe you will be positioned to understand your Bible from covenant perspective, relate with God based on covenant, and be in a position to build on the revelation contained in this book.

One of the lamentations in the bible was about Ephraim. Psalm 78:9-11 says:

"The children of Ephraim, being armed and carrying bows, turned back in the day of battle. They did not keep the covenant of God; They refused to walk in His law and forgot His works and His wonders that He had shown them."

The children of Ephraim had all the ammunition they needed but they turned back on the day of battle. Why? They did not keep the covenant of God and as the Message Translation puts it: *"They were cowards to God's Covenant, refused to walk by his Word. They forgot what he had done— marvels he'd done right before their eyes..."* You can only keep what you know. They forgot God's covenant and were cowards towards it.

As we grow in our knowledge of God and His covenant with us, we grow bold in dealing with daily life matters; we are more confident in our prayers; and our expectation levels in the promises of God become higher.

I am excited about this book. I have reviewed it and reviewed it hoping I have been able by the grace of God, to put into writing what I have in my spirit. I pray you are as excited about what you have been exposed to in this book as I am.

To reach out to me on any questions, comments, or your personal views, email me on connect@niyiolujobi.org.

May we all experience the fullness of the God covenant in our lives and in our families in Jesus' name.

Niyi Olujobi

CHAPTER ONE

WHAT IS COVENANT?

"And as they did eat, Jesus took bread, and blessed, and brake it, and gave to them, and said, Take, eat this is my body. And he took the cup, and when he had given thanks, he gave it to them: and they all drank of it. And he said unto them, this is my blood of the New Testament, which is shed for many. Verily I say unto you, I will drink no more of the fruit of the vine, until that day that I drink it new in the kingdom of God. And when they had sung a hymn, they went out into the mount of Olives." ***(Mark 14:22-26).***

This text is often read when believers are about to receive Holy Communion. It is usually the central text read because it tells us about the Last Supper, the occasion when the Lord Jesus instituted the Holy Communion rite. However, I want us to have a better look at it, so I'll only highlight one or two points before delving into the next scripture.

When Jesus passed the cup of wine to his disciples, and said, 'This is the blood of the new covenant, is it not quite interesting that none of the disciples asked Him, 'What is the new covenant?', 'Why blood?' or 'Why a new covenant?' The reason why they didn't ask any of these questions is that they were familiar with the concept of blood covenants. But I'm not exactly sure how much they understood the concept of a new covenant. The fact that he said, 'this is the blood of the new covenant', connotes that there was already an existing or old covenant. So, when Jesus was speaking to this bunch of Jewish guys who esteemed covenants and perhaps understood them very well in theory and is saying that he is creating a new covenant, they must have understood the word 'covenant', but whether they understood the word "new" is a different ball game altogether.

Jesus' original audience at the time was being told that a new covenant was soon going to be enacted and that they were going to be partakers of this new covenant. All of those who witnessed the Last Supper partook of this meal, which was symbolic of his flesh and blood, knowing that they were entering into a covenant. There are other kinds of covenants that may exist, but when it comes to a blood covenant, it is a lot more permanent and binding, and its implications are much stronger than other kinds of covenant. It was a blood covenant that was being established that blessed day at the Lord's Supper and each one of them decided to partake of this covenant.

However, the enaction of the new does not necessarily mean that the old is totally discarded. What that word "new" from the original Greek definition suggests is a better (or second) covenant compared to the already existing one. I can guess that everyone would want something better than what they currently have. If I asked you whether you wanted a better car than the one in your parking lot, your answer would probably be a yes. Do you want a better house? I can almost hear your enthusiastic yes!

Let's also look at the root meaning of the word 'covenant'. Covenant is derived from the Hebrew root word *beriyṯ*: A noun meaning covenant, treaty, alliance, or agreement. This word describes covenants, or agreements between and among human beings e.g., between Abraham and the Amorites, Abraham and the Philistines, Jacob, and Laban, etc. (Gen. 14:13; 21:27, 32; 31:44). This word is also used to describe God making a covenant with humankind e.g., God's covenant with Noah (Gen. 9:11-13, 15-17; Isa. 54:10); with Abraham, Isaac, and Jacob (Gen. 15:18; 17:2, 4, 7, 9-11, 13, 14, 19, 21), and Moses at Sinai (Ex. 19:5; 24:7 & 8; 34:10; Deut. 29:1 [28:69]). The word *beriyṯ* is often preceded by the verb *karaṯ* to express the technical idea of "cutting a covenant."

In Greek, covenant comes from the root word: *diathḗkē*; which means testament, or covenant. It is a solemn disposition, institution, or apportionment of God to man (Heb. 9:16-18) to which our word "dispensation" answers adequately, e.g., for the dispensation or institution which God appointed to Abraham and the patriarchs (Acts 3:25); the dispensation from Sinai (Heb. 8:9); the dispensation of faith and free justification of which Christ is the mediator (Heb. 7:22; 8:6). It means a covenant, but not in the sense that God came to an agreement or compromise with the fallen man as if signing a contract. Rather, it involves the declaration of God's promise to make Abraham and his seed the recipients of certain blessings (Gen. 13:14-17; 15:18; 17:7-8, 19-21; 21:12, 14; 22:2, 12) or the Sinaitic *diathḗkē* to Moses, which was a conditional dispensation or series of promises (Ex. 19:5-8, 20-23; Heb. 12:18-21) that God made for the Jews only if they obeyed.

When our Lord Jesus, as recorded and reported by the Apostle Paul in 1 Cor. 11:25, said, *"This cup is the New Testament in my blood,"* the word was used as will or promise. It was the fulfillment of His promise. Our Lord here was almost in the very presence of death and, in view of that death, He activated the will or the promise, vividly promising His disciples a share in His inheritance (Luke 22:29). The promise as we see in Luke 22:29 was His kingdom.

*"And I bestow upon you a kingdom, just as My Father bestowed one upon Me" (**Luke 22:29**)*

8 Relevant Points About Covenants

1. Covenants are always cut. Biblical covenants usually involve the shedding of blood. So, when the Bible uses the phrase, 'and the Lord established a covenant', what the Lord is saying is that I am arising to make a covenant, to fulfill, to establish, or to activate a covenant. However, the most important point to note is that covenants are cut.

Genesis 15 is a good illustration of God's covenant with Abram with the shedding of blood.

"And he said, "Lord God, how shall I know that I will inherit it?" So, He said to him, "Bring Me a three-year-old heifer, a three-year-old female goat, a three-year-old ram, a turtledove, and a young pigeon." Then he brought all these to Him and cut them in two, down the middle, and placed each piece opposite the other; but he did not cut the birds in two." (**Genesis 15:8-10**)

Abram had just received a promise from the Lord with assurance. God took him to look at the sky and number the stars which he couldn't. Abram believed in God, and it was accounted to him as righteousness. To enter into covenant with Abram, God requested a heifer, goat, ram, turtledove, and a pigeon. God cut these animals, except for the birds in two – down the middle. That would have been a very bloody space. The end of this encounter was that God cut a covenant with Abram. *"On the same day the Lord made a covenant with Abram…"* (**v18**)

2. A covenant between God and man is usually initiated by God. It is usually God's initiative. It is usually God who comes to man and says, 'I am making a covenant with you.' Think about the Noahic covenant, the Abrahamic covenant, the Mosaic covenant, or the Davidic covenant. Every one of these covenants was initiated by God.

Noahic Covenant:

"Then God spoke to Noah and to his sons with him, saying: "And as for Me, behold, I establish My covenant with you and with your descendants after you, and with every living creature that is with you: the birds, the cattle, and every beast of the earth with you, of all that go out of the ark, every beast of the earth. Thus, I establish My covenant with you: Never again shall all flesh be cut off by the waters of the flood; never again shall there be a flood to destroy the earth.""" (***Genesis 9:8-11***)

3. Covenants usually require the participation of both parties. I have heard many say that some of God's covenant is unconditional. I tend to look at this differently from others. Except for the Noahic Covenant, every covenant of God with man requires the man's response, obedience, and/or doing something. When a covenant is established between you and God, God does His bit, and you are expected to do yours too to keep the covenant. In Genesis 17:9, the Lord said to Abraham, *'As for you, you shall keep My covenant'*. This means that Abraham had a responsibility to keep the covenant already established between him and God. In the same vein, when you and I say that we are in a covenant with the Lord, we should note that there are responsibilities that accompany the covenant.

Taking the Abraham's example, a step further, when God said to Abraham to keep His covenant, what did God mean by that?

"This is My covenant which you shall keep, between Me and you and your descendants after you: Every male child among you shall be circumcised; and you shall be circumcised in the flesh of your foreskins, and it shall be a sign of the covenant between Me and you. He who is eight days old among you shall be circumcised, every male child in your generations, he who is born in your house or bought

with money from any foreigner who is not your descendant. He who is born in your house and he who is bought with your money must be circumcised, and My covenant shall be in your flesh for an everlasting covenant. And the uncircumcised male child, who is not circumcised in the flesh of his foreskin, that person shall be cut off from his people; he has broken My covenant." (**Genesis 17:10-14**)

Verse 14 made it clear that an uncircumcised male child has broken God's covenant. They may be biologically related to Abraham and the covenant could be available to them by right however, they have the responsibility to be circumcised before partaking in this covenant.

A good example will be Moses:

In Exodus 4:24-26, the scriptures say *"And it came to pass on the way, at the encampment, that the Lord met him and sought to kill him. Then Zipporah took a sharp stone and cut off the foreskin of her son and cast it at Moses' feet, and said, "Surely you are a husband of blood to me!" So, He let him go. Then she said, "You are a husband of blood!"—because of the circumcision."*

I hope you understand what happened here. Prior to this event, Moses had encountered God who told him, 'You are going to the children of Israel. You're going to deliver them from their affliction'. But Moses was married to Zipporah who was not a covenanted woman. So, they had two sons, who have not been circumcised. Remember that Moses was a member of the Abrahamic lineage, but his sons were now outside the covenant because they have not been circumcised. God then said to Moses, 'You can't go and do the assignments I gave you if you will not circumcise your son'.

Moses became very sick, almost to the point of death, and this is why the Bible said that God wanted to kill him. Moses knew why he was sick, and when Zipporah was told the reason for Moses' illness, she decided that they were going to circumcise their boys. Circumcision is bloody and that is why she called him the husband of blood. However, if the rite had not been carried out, Moses would have been in the covenant while his sons remained outside the covenant.

God attached the condition of Moses' sons being circumcised as one of the qualifications for Moses to resume his role as a covenant leader of the children of Israel. So, we all have to realize that as God makes covenants with us, we have our responsibilities toward these established covenants. These responsibilities are not limited to us; our families and children also have a responsibility to walk in the covenant and meet its requirements.

4. God's covenant always includes a blessing. God told Abraham, *'I will make you exceedingly fruitful, and I will make nations of you and kings shall come from you.'* (Genesis 17:6). There is a blessing that accompanies any covenant between you and God. I'm not talking about blessings with an 's' but 'The Blessing' from which blessings spring up. Deuteronomy 28 talks about the blessing being upon you. It was not referring to the many blessings like a good job, a nice car, a loving spouse, riches, etc. but The Blessing which is a part of the covenant God had with the children of Israel and us, today. When God makes a covenant, there is always the blessing that follows the covenant.

I love to read about covenants in the Bible and I decided to put this set of verses here to reveal how God blessed David in the Davidic covenant of which we are also partakers.

*"My covenant I will not break, nor alter the word that has gone out of My lips. Once I have sworn by My holiness; I will not lie to David: His seed shall endure forever, and his throne as the sun before Me; It shall be established forever like the moon, even like the faithful witness in the sky." Selah" (***Psalm 89:34-37***)*

Read the whole of Psalm 89. I promise you will be blessed.

5. A covenant with God includes promises which are multifaceted. There are many of God's promises in the Bible, and in most cases, they are always promises attached to covenants. When studying the covenants of which you are a partaker (mainly, the Abrahamic Covenant and the New Covenant), you must study and understand the promises that are attached to these covenants, because the covenant being fulfilled is a promise being fulfilled in your life. Hebrews 8:6 says:

"But now He has obtained a more excellent ministry, inasmuch as He is also Mediator of a better covenant, which was established on better promises." (**Hebrews 8:6**)

It is our responsibility to understand the better covenant which has been cut on our behalf and the better promises which are for us based on the better covenant, that we might know how to appropriate them.

6. Covenants with God are usually multi-generational. God does not establish covenants that end with one generation. When He was talking with Abraham in Genesis 17:7, He said, '*the covenant that I'm making right now will be with you and your descendants and their generations for an everlasting covenant.*' So, it's a covenant that did not just end with Abraham, rather it continued with Isaac, Jacob, the children of Israel, Christ, and all of us who are now grafted into the same covenant. It is a multi-generational covenant. When the Davidic Covenant said in Psalm 89 *"I have made a covenant with My chosen, I have sworn to My servant David: 'Your seed I will establish forever and build up your throne to all generations.'" Selah" (vv3-4)*; the covenant was not just with David alone but on his seed and his children that followed after. So, God's covenants are multi-generational. If God appears to you and says he's making a covenant with you, which He can, the covenant will not be limited to you, but it will rub off on your children and your children's children, transcending many generations that will come after you because the Word of the Lord will go ahead of you.

7. Covenant may require a change of name. I'm not saying it always does, but sometimes a change of name happens to seal a covenant. In the Abrahamic covenant, not only did Abram's name change to Abraham, but the name of God equally was now attached to his new name, Abraham. Invariably, we see that Abram became Abraham. But when you go to the Hebrew roots, you will discover the fact that Abram was attached to the word Ha, a word that is derived from the word 'Abba'. So, God gave Abraham His name and attached it to his original name. This is how Abram became Abraham. I know we tend to interpret Abram to mean exalted father, and Abraham to mean father of many nations. I am not opposing this fact. My point, however, is this: the 'ha' that was added, was the name of God and it became a seal of the covenant. From that day onwards, God became the God of Abraham. There was nothing like the 'God of Abraham' before Abraham was born neither was there anything like that when Abraham was a child or in his formative years. The Bible never even called Him the God of Abram. He is the God of Abraham. When God gave Abraham a new name, He too had a new name. We also see this event of name change in marriages today, at least in some communities. In such communities, the wife takes the name of the husband because they have entered into a covenant. In this book, by the grace of God, we will touch on covenants in the area of marriage and various other areas of life to help you understand that your life itself is woven in covenants, and some of us have entered into covenants with things that we must break off from. Your parents may have entered some covenants that you need to deal with. So, it's very important that we understand the concept and power of the covenant.

8. **In covenant, there is an exchange and bonding.** When blood covenants are cut between humans or covenants that exist between God and man, there is usually an exchange. An exchange of strengths and weaknesses; an exchange of resources; an exchange of positions etc. The stronger one in the covenant takes on the weakness of the other and vice versa. We will get into further details in this book however, for quick illustration, we take a glimpse at David and Jonathan who entered into a covenant together exchanging armor to signify the entering of the covenant.

*"Then Jonathan and David made a covenant because he loved him as his own soul. And Jonathan took off the robe that was on him and gave it to David, with his armor, even to his sword and his bow and his belt." (**1 Samuel 18:3-4**)*

As we study their lives, we can understand Jonathan's position in defending and protecting David. David will later reciprocate by extending the covenant blessing to Jonathan's son – Mephibosheth.

Perhaps, this will make us understand Paul's statement to the church in Corinth with regard to the covenant exchanges we have with our Lord Jesus Christ.

*"For you know the grace of our Lord Jesus Christ, that though He was rich, yet for your sakes He became poor, that you through His poverty might become rich." (**2 Corinthians 8:9**)*

We will further explore covenant exchanges as we go through this book.

CHAPTER TWO

THE ABRAHAMIC COVENANT

"On the same day the Lord made a covenant with Abram..." (***Genesis 15:18a***)

Learning what the Word says from a covenant perspective should be the duty of every believer in Christ, and my prayer is that your eyes will continually see what is, and what has been made available to you through covenants.

There are two main covenants that are crucial for believers today to understand in detail. They are:

1. **The Abrahamic Covenant**
2. **The New Covenant**

In this chapter, we shall be looking into the Abrahamic covenant. Both covenants are still very relevant today for every believer in Christ. It's important that you understand these covenants so that you can rightly steward them in your life.

"When Abram was ninety-nine years old, the Lord appeared to Abram and said to him, "I am Almighty God; walk before Me and be blameless. And I will make My covenant between Me and you and will multiply you exceedingly." Then Abram fell on his face, and God talked with him, saying: "As for Me, behold, My covenant is with you, and you shall be a father of many nations. No longer shall your name be called Abram, but your name shall be Abraham; for I have

made you a father of many nations. I will make you exceedingly fruitful; and I will make nations of you, and kings shall come from you. And I will establish My covenant between Me and you and your descendants after you in their generations, for an everlasting covenant, to be God to you and your descendants after you. Also, I give to you and your descendants after you the land in which you are a stranger, all the land of Canaan, as an everlasting possession; and I will be their God."" ***(Genesis 17:1-8).***

For I have made you a father of many nations

By virtue of what God said to Abraham in Genesis 15 and 17, God made a covenant with Abraham and declared that he would be the father of many nations. This covenant was not halfhearted or partial, but a total bond between the Lord and Abraham. The Lord asked for everything from Abraham, including himself and all that he owned, and in return, everything that is God and all that belongs to God would also belong to Abraham. This means that Abraham, his children, and his possessions all belong to the Lord, and conversely, everything that is the Lord belongs to Abraham. This covenant relationship is a total commitment, with Abraham and the Lord both sworn to one another as senior covenant partners.

In Genesis 15, in the beginning, in verse one, the Bible said, the word of the Lord came to Abram in a vision, saying, "Do not be afraid, Abram. I am your shield, your exceedingly great reward."

Abram at the time was concerned about being childless, but the Lord reassured him by pointing out the stars and promising that his descendants would be as numerous as the stars. Abraham believed in the Lord and this faith was credited to him as righteousness.

Now, what the phrase "believed in the Lord" actually means he believed in the Lord. It wasn't just the statement (or word) that

God said he would have descendants that would fill the entire earth. The word "believe" in the original language means that Abraham decided to give his entire being to God. He gave his entirety to God.

He decided to give everything in total commitment. It was a total giveaway and a total abandonment, as he abandoned himself to God. He believed that God would fulfill His promise, but it was more than just belief in that specific promise. Abraham gave everything to God, including himself. God then gave Abraham His righteousness, which was imputed to Abraham as righteousness. You can say there is a different level of believing i.e., from believing in the promise to believing in the Promiser. Abram believed in the Lord. This is why Galatians 3 says that even before the law was given, God preached the gospel to Abraham. And because Abraham believed it, it was credited to him as righteousness.

"And the Scripture, foreseeing that God would justify the Gentiles by faith, preached the gospel to Abraham beforehand, saying, "In you all the nations shall be blessed." (***Galatians 3:8***)

Now, this righteousness that we receive today is a gift from God through grace, not something that we earn through our own efforts (See Ephesians 2). Abraham received this gift of righteousness (which is part of the God-nature or virtue. Righteousness is a core virtue and nature of God. God is called Jehovah Tsidkenu - The Lord Our Righteousness (Jeremiah 33:16)), although he was not part of the new covenant so that he could be the father of both the circumcised and the uncircumcised (Jews and Gentiles). So, if God credited righteousness to Abraham as a gift, today we receive righteousness as a gift from God having believed in Christ (Romans 5:17), then, the extent of Abram's commitment to the Lord and believing the Lord should also be our extent as well.

As we read the Abrahamic covenant further in Genesis 17, we see the condition stated by God to belong to this covenant irrespective of being Abraham's biological or bloodline descendants.

"And God said to Abraham: "As for you, you shall keep My covenant, you, and your descendants after you throughout their generations. This is My covenant which you shall keep, between Me and you and your descendants after you: Every male child among you shall be circumcised; and you shall be circumcised in the flesh of your foreskins, and it shall be a sign of the covenant between Me and you. He who is eight days old among you shall be circumcised, every male child in your generations, he who is born in your house or bought with money from any foreigner who is not your descendant. He who is born in your house and he who is bought with your money must be circumcised, and My covenant shall be in your flesh for an everlasting covenant. And the uncircumcised male child, who is not circumcised in the flesh of his foreskin, that person shall be cut off from his people; he has broken My covenant." (**vv9-14**)

It is therefore important to note that for any of Abraham's descendants to claim they belong to the covenant, they must be circumcised. This is because circumcision becomes the sign of the covenant. The sign of the covenant is not the same as the covenant itself. God told Abraham that the part he and his descendants must play in terms of the sign is to be circumcised. Today, circumcision is of the heart, not of the flesh.

In Genesis 17:13, the Bible says that anyone born in Abraham's house or bought with money must be circumcised and that the covenant will be in their flesh as an everlasting covenant. This means that even those whom Abraham bought as slaves could become part of the covenant by being circumcised. God is making provisions for not just Abraham's biological children, but also those who enter his household for any reason to be able to partake in the covenant that Abraham is a part of. However, the sign of the covenant for all males is circumcision.

The law came later through Moses, but before the law came, Abraham, Isaac, Jacob, and the children of Israel were governed by the covenant. They didn't have a law, statutes, or an oath, and they relied on the covenant to guide their actions. Despite the addition of the law, the covenant remained in place and the law merely provided a structure for the nation. The children of Israel were expected to fully give themselves to the Lord and live their lives according to His direction, even without specific laws or regulations before the law came into force.

Abraham knew that he was in a covenant with God and that God was in a covenant with him and his descendants. This meant that everything in his life belonged to God. If we want to say that we are in the covenant today, we must be fully committed to it and cannot have any part of our lives that is not included in the covenant. The covenant with God requires us to give ourselves fully to it, as Abraham did. God tested Abraham's commitment to living in the covenant and Abraham passed the test.

In Genesis 22:1-2, it is stated that God tested Abraham. In these verses, God asks Abraham to take his son Isaac, whom he loves, and offer him as a burnt offering on one of the mountains in the land of Moriah. Abraham was aware that he was in a covenant with God when this request was made.

God knew that the covenant he made with Abraham would be fulfilled. Abraham spent 25 years, and likely even more before that, trusting in God's promise to give him a child. In an effort to fulfill this promise, Abraham fathered a son, Ishmael, with Hagar. However, this was not the promised child. In Genesis 17, God tells Abraham that his wife Sarah will bear him a son and that they should name him Isaac. Abraham laughs at this, as he was over 100 years of age, and he did not think it was possible for him to have children.

It was a miracle child, and he was not possible in the natural world. But because God said it, and because there is a covenant partner in God, nothing is impossible.

Abraham knew the significance of being in a covenant because, in their culture, a covenant meant that their lives were bound to each other. If one person made a covenant with another, their lives were also bound together. Isaac, the children of Gerar, and others understood this concept as well.

In Genesis 26, Isaac was stronger than the people of the land. The king came to him and suggested that they make a covenant so that the blessings on Isaac would also be on them. The people of the land wanted to be able to sow and reap a hundredfold and to have wells with water like Isaac's. They knew Isaac was no ordinary person. Abimelech said at first:

"Go away from us, for you are much mightier than we." (**v16**)

Then he realized it is wisdom to make a covenant with this covenanted person and then, he said:

"We have certainly seen that the Lord is with you. So, we said, 'Let there now be an oath between us, between you and us; and let us make a covenant with you, that you will do us no harm, since we have not touched you, and since we have done nothing to you but good and have sent you away in peace. You are now the blessed of the Lord.'" (**vv28-29**)

Isaac agreed to the covenant. It is foolish to fight against someone who is in a covenant with God because the blessings on them can also come to you. The people of the land fought against Isaac for the first two wells but, when they saw that he had found water at the third well, they realized that there was no point in fighting against him because he was greater than them. This was due to Abraham's (Isaac's father) covenant with God.

Back to Genesis 22 where God will test Abraham regarding the covenant, God commanded Abraham to offer his son Isaac as a sacrifice. Abraham obeyed without hesitation because of the covenant he had with God. God knew that the sacrifice would not be completed and that he was simply testing Abraham's faith and devotion to the covenant. The word "tested" in this context suggests that God was examining Abraham's faith and loyalty to him. Abraham's willingness to follow God's command, even in the face of such a difficult and seemingly impossible task, shows the depth of his faith and the strength of the covenant between him and God.

Then Abraham arose, took the boy, the wood for the burnt offering, and his servants, and journeyed to the place where God had told him to go. And Abraham believed in his heart that God would raise his son from the dead, as stated in the book of Hebrews.

"By faith Abraham, when he was tested, offered up Isaac, and he who had received the promises offered up his only begotten son, of whom it was said, "In Isaac your seed shall be called," concluding that God was able to raise him up, even from the dead, from which he also received him in a figurative sense." (**Hebrews 11:17-19**)

Though there is no record of God raising anyone from the dead at that time, Abraham knew his covenant partner well enough to trust that even if he offered his son as a sacrifice, God would raise him from the dead. Hebrews 11 tells us that this belief was in Abraham's heart.

When Abraham took his son to offer him as a sacrifice, he was about to slay him with a knife when the Angel of the Lord called to him from heaven. The Angel of the Lord is often considered a reference to God himself, as in the Trinity. The Angel said to Abraham, *"Do not lay your hand on the lad, or do anything to him; for now, I know that you fear God, since you have not withheld your son, your only son, from Me.".'* (Genesis 22:12) In other words, God was telling Abraham that he had found a man who was faithful to his covenant, and who feared God enough to follow his commands even when it was difficult. This story is often used to illustrate the faith and obedience of Abraham and the faithfulness of God to his people. God has found His covenant-keeping man.

Abraham had a choice when God commanded him to offer his son as a sacrifice. He could have chosen to defy God and refuse to offer his son, and he could have repented and begged for forgiveness. But instead, Abraham chose to obey God and offer his son as a sacrifice, because he understood the covenant he had with God and knew that God would fulfill his end of the bargain. Abraham was about 118 years old at the time and his son was about 18, so it's likely that the father was not physically stronger than the son. However, the son also had faith in God and trusted in the God of his father. This story is often used to illustrate the depth of Abraham's faith and his willingness to trust and obey God, even when it was difficult.

Isaac would have said: "I will lay on this altar, let my head be cut off, let my throat be slit because I trust in the God of my father." I need you to understand how covenant works here. You see, that was a total commitment from Abraham. If God had asked for Abraham himself to be sacrificed, who was already 118 years old, it would not have been much of a sacrifice. But what God asked for was much more precious - the apple of Abraham's eye, Isaac. And by asking for Isaac, God was asking for Abraham's total commitment. God's response was: "now I know that you are a man who keeps his covenant, Abraham." God went on to say in verse 16 to 18, *"By Myself I have sworn, says the Lord, because you have done this thing, and have not withheld your son, your only son— blessing I will bless you, and multiplying I will multiply your descendants as the stars of the heaven and as the sand which is on the seashore; and your descendants shall possess the gate of their enemies. In your seed all the nations of the earth shall be blessed, because you have obeyed My voice."* We can paraphrase and say, because you are a covenant-keeping man, Abraham, in your seed, all nations of the earth shall be blessed.

He said, 'I swear, God doesn't need to swear. But in this situation, I don't know of any other place where God swore. God said by myself, that is to say, by my throne, except I cease to be God. This covenant will stand except I stop being God because he found a man who can keep the covenant. As I studied this, I realized that the reason why God appeared to Isaac and said not to go to Egypt was because of the covenant with his father. The reason why he preserved Jacob, even on his journey to the house of Laban, was because he had a covenant with their father Abraham. The reason why the children of Israel were a special nation was because of the covenant of Abraham.

I realized that in everything that had happened to the children of Israel, even though they were rebellious, God did not forget the covenant. He would punish them, allow enemies to conquer them, and do other things when they are disobedient or break the terms of the covenant, but he would still bring them back because of the covenant that was in place. As I meditated on this, I looked at the Old Covenant and realized that in this covenant, God said none of them would be sick. He made it clear in the book of Exodus, saying, 'I am the Lord that heals you.' He said, 'I am your Jehovah Rapha,' meaning 'I am the surety of your health.' I'm thinking that this is God speaking to a people, asking who they will trust: scientists, doctors, or the Almighty God in heaven, who guarantees their health. Who will you trust?

The Bible teaches us that the children of Israel spent 40 years in the wilderness and, according to the Scriptures, none of them were feeble. This is remarkable considering the barren, desert conditions they faced, where there was no food or vegetation. Yet God provided for them through the covenant He had made with them, raining down food from heaven and bringing water from a rock to sustain them. He also protected them, giving them a pillar of cloud by day to shield them from the scorching sun and a pillar of fire by night to keep them warm. All of these provisions were given to them through the covenant God had made with them.

The Bible tells us that God made a covenant with the children of Israel and promised that none of them would be barren or suffer miscarriages. This is exemplified in Exodus 23:26, where God says, "there shall be none barren among you." Even those who seemed old, such as Sarah and Abraham, were given children through this covenant. The only exception mentioned in the Bible is the wife of David, the daughter of Saul, who became barren and died without children. However, for those who keep the covenant, God promises that they will not be barren or suffer miscarriages. This is a reminder of the power and protection provided by the covenant that God has made with His people.

We may not have been aware before, but now you know. The enemy might look to take advantage of your ignorance but now, you know. Now, we know and because we know, we must stand on what we know. We have the same covenant, Hallelujah. There is no army that can defeat us. Even the greatest power at the time of Moses, the Egyptian empire with a king almost worshiped like a god, could not stop them from leaving the country. The kings they encountered on the way could not overcome them because of the covenant, although they had no weapons.

They are just a group of slaves who don't know how to fight. Even Joshua, who seemed like the warrior amongst them, couldn't win battles on his own. He only won when Moses raised his hand. That's not really fighting. The one on the mountain is the one winning the battle. When Moses' hand got tired, Aaron and Hur held it up so they could continue to win. Joshua may come back and say they fought well and won, but that's not the case. The covenant ensures that they don't lose. The only defeat I can think of right now was in Ai, and that was because someone broke the instructions in Jericho. I'm talking about the Abrahamic covenant and how as a covenanted people of God, we need to understand it in order to maximize it.

Think about how strong the Midianites were in Gideon's time. They couldn't defeat Gideon, and Gideon didn't even have a weapon. But when God narrowed Gideon's army down to just 300, do you know what he gave them to fight with? A torch and a horn. They went to battle against an army with just a torch and a horn, and they won. Glory to God.

We may not have known before, but now we know, and we will not lose any battles again. We won't lose any battles again because now we know. I need you to understand this because when you know that you have a covenant partner who stands for you and your covenant partner is God, you can't be afraid. You can't be afraid because you know that the covenant works. It doesn't matter.

Jehoshaphat and his people had no weapons. Then, three kings came and said they were going to wipe out Judah. Jehoshaphat went with the people to the temple of God and said, *"O Lord God of our fathers, are You not God in heaven, and do You not rule over all the kingdoms of the nations, and in Your hand is there not power and might, so that no one is able to withstand You? Are You not our God, who drove out the inhabitants of this land before Your people Israel, and gave it to the descendants of Abraham Your friend forever?"* (**2 Chronicles 20:6-7**).

He went back to Abraham and the covenant in his appeal to God. I need you to read some stories in the Bible about how the Lord always delivers His people. How He delivered them from Egypt, how He performed miracles for them, and how He promised, 'I will never leave you nor forsake you.'

Now, they were in the situation they were in. Then, a voice from the back said (in my paraphrase), "Jehoshaphat, calm down. You are in a covenant. The battle is not yours". You see, the battle is not yours and is not just a casual statement being made. It is made of the covenant. 'The battle is not yours' means that I will fight your battles. It means that you don't need to respond. I'll respond on your behalf. If God fights for you, who can ever defeat you? Come on.

When God says, 'No matter where they come from, let them gather together because their gathering is not of me. I will scatter them for your sake. He is saying that He is the one who makes the blacksmith and the one who blows the coal. He will make sure that no matter what they do, they cannot win the battle because He is for you, and you are His covenant child.

You are the one that I made the covenant with. I saw you in Abraham, I saw you when I was entering the covenant, I saw you when I was cutting the covenant. I knew that you would go through what you are going through. I am the Almighty God. I watch over my word to perform it. I will never break my covenant, nor will I turn back from the word that I have spoken. Because I have said it, I will do it. I am the mighty man of war.

Where are the Egyptians today? They are under the Red Sea. Where are those who stood against Jehovah God? I say they are dead today because they cannot fight against the covenant children of God. The Lord said to Moses, 'Go tell Pharaoh, "Israel is my firstborn. You touch my firstborn; I will touch your firstborn."'

"Then you shall say to Pharaoh, 'Thus says the Lord: "Israel is My son, My firstborn. So, I say to you, let My son go that he may serve Me. But if you refuse to let him go, indeed I will kill your son, your firstborn."'" (**Exodus 4:22-23**)

When Pharaoh didn't get the message and kept persecuting the firstborn of God, God had to kill his firstborn to release His own.

I declare today, no matter the battle, no matter the fight, because you are a covenant child of God, He will arise on your behalf and every gang up will be scattered in the name of Jesus. Amen. Because of the covenant.

CHAPTER THREE

THE NEW COVENANT

And as they were eating, Jesus took bread, blessed, and broke it, and gave it to the disciples and said, "Take, eat; this is My body. "Then He took the cup, and gave thanks, and gave it to them, saying, "Drink from it, all of you. For this is My blood of the new covenant, which is shed for many for the remission of sins. But I say to you, I will not drink of this fruit of the vine from now on until that day when I drink it new with you in My Father's kingdom. And when they had sung a hymn, they went out to the Mount of Olives **(Matthew 26:26-30).**

Jesus was having dinner with His disciples. He took bread, blessed it, broke it, and said, this is my body. Now, did they understand what he was saying? Perhaps

Then he goes on and said, *"This cup that is filled with wine, take it, and drink. This is my blood."* They drank it, knowing that they were entering into a covenant with Jesus. They understood what the covenant meant. And when they were partaking of it, they knew that they were cutting a covenant with Jesus, and the Father, therefore, they, Jesus, and the Father are now one. The strength of the Father and the Son is now available to them because of the covenant Jesus had with them.

This covenant cutting would have made sense to the disciples as they heard Jesus' prayer in John 17 declaring the oneness of His disciples, Himself, and the Father. The cutting of the New Covenant with His disciples made Him one with them and before their very eyes, they see the fulfillment of that prayer.

"I do not pray for these alone, but also for those who will believe in Me through their word; that they all may be one, as You, Father, are in Me, and I in You; that they also may be one in Us, that the world may believe that You sent Me." (**John 17:20-21**)

How can they be one without a covenant? The covenant brought them into that oneness.

It's difficult to do the math, because how would you say, "The Father is in the Son, the Son is in the Father". But it's what Jesus said. The new covenant made you one with God and His Son, Jesus Christ.

"And the glory which You gave Me I have given them, that they may be one just as We are one: I in them, and You in Me; that they may be made perfect in one, and that the world may know that You have sent Me, and have loved them as You have loved Me. "Father, I desire that they also whom You gave Me may be with Me where I am, that they may behold My glory which You have given Me; for You loved Me before the foundation of the world." (**vv22-24**)

This new covenant brings you into oneness with God. When you enter into a covenant with Jesus, it is no longer the case that the presence of God will just dwell temporarily, as it used to do prior to this covenant. Now, it is a covenant that makes us one. You become one with God and enter into a place where God is directly your father, just as he is Jesus's Father.

Important notable points:

The New Covenant did not make the Abrahamic Covenant obsolete. Rather, it was the furtherance or the fulfillment of it.

God said through His Angel to Abraham, *"Abraham, through your seed, all the nations of the earth will be blessed."* (**Genesis 22:18**)

In Galatians 3:16, we realized seed that the seed is Christ. "*Now to Abraham and his seed were the promises made. He does not say, "And to seeds," as of many, but as of one, "and to your seed", who is Christ* ***(Galatians 3:16).***

The Lord made a promise to Abraham by covenant saying, by your seed all nations of the earth will be blessed. That Seed is Christ who is the fulfillment of the covenant word of promise spoken to him. Therefore, this does not nullify the Abrahamic covenant; it rather fulfills and empowers it.

The new covenant made the Mosaic Covenant of no effect. Two scriptures will make that clear. *And this I say that the law, which was four hundred and thirty years later, cannot annul the covenant that was confirmed before by God in Christ. That it should make promise of promise of no effect* ***(Galatians 3: 17-18).***

God cut a covenant with Abraham long before Moses or the law came to being. The Mosaic Law, which came 430 years later, cannot cancel the promises that God made to Abraham before Moses. If the inheritance was based on the law, it would not be a promise from God, but since God gave it to Abraham by promise, it is not based on the law. In Hebrews 8, we can further understand the New Covenant.

For if the first covenant had been faultless, then no place would have been sought for a second, because finding fault with them. He says "Behold, the days are coming, says the Lord, when I will make a new covenant with the house of Israel and with the house of Judah. not according to the covenant, I made with their fathers in the day when I took them by the hand to lead them out of the land of Egypt; because they did not continue in my covenant, and I disregarded them, says the Lord ***(Hebrews 8:7-9).***

Now, what covenant was enacted or put in place when the children of Israel were led out of Egypt? It was the Mosaic covenant. The Bible records that this second or new covenant is "*not according to the covenant I [God] made with their fathers in the day when I [God] took them by the hand to lead them out of the land of Egypt*" and God disregarded them and the covenant because they did not continue in it.

*For this is the covenant that I will make with the house of Israel after those days, says the Lord: I will put my laws in their mind and write them on their hearts; and I will be their God, and they shall be my people. None of them shall teach his neighbor and none his brother saying, know the Lord, for all shall know me from the least of them to the greatest of them, For I will be merciful to their unrighteousness, and their sin and lawless deeds I will remember no more. In he says "A new covenant" he has made the first obsolete. Now what is becoming obsolete and growing old is ready to vanish away (**Hebrews 8:10-13**).*

A new covenant has made the first (old) obsolete. Now, what is becoming obsolete and growing old is ready to vanish away! The Old Covenant which is the Mosaic Covenant is now obsolete and has vanished away.

Where the confusion comes for many of us, is the term "Old Testament" and what it means. Is Old Testament (testament means covenant) Genesis to Malachi in the Bible? Is the Old Testament (covenant) the covenant of Moses? It is the latter. We should not be confused with the manner in which our Bibles are categorized but rather follow the revelation of the word.

The Old Testament is the Mosaic Covenant or Law of Moses. Before the law came, there were people existing and there were covenants that God enacted before the law came. So, the law did not come to annul the covenant that existed before it came but to guide the people until the promised Seed comes.

The promised Seed has come.

Why was the law given?

*What purpose then does the law serve? It was added because of transgressions, till the Seed should come to whom the promise was made; and it was appointed through angels by the hand of a mediator. Now a mediator does not mediate for one only, but God is one. Is the law then against the promises of God? Certainly not! For if there had been a law given which could have given life, truly righteousness would have been by the law (**Galatians 3:19-21**).*

We need to understand dispensations and what God is saying now.

The purpose of the law was to serve as a temporary measure until the arrival of the Seed, Christ. When Christ came, the law became unnecessary because God becomes the witness in our hearts to his law. The law without the spirit of the law made the law inferior. When the spirit of the law is applied to, for example, the ten commandments, we see the revelation Jesus brought in the gospels applying the "spirit" to the "law". Jesus said that if you look at a woman lustfully, you have already committed adultery. The law is inferior to the grace and standard of the Son.

Now, many people run around and say grace, grace, grace, grace covers everything and allows them to do whatever they want. And they believe that grace covers all their sins. I'm not saying that God does not forgive sins. He does and he tells us to come to him for forgiveness. But the issue is this: can you continue to sin and expect grace to abound? The standard has become higher because God says it's not just about following a list of do's and don'ts. He wants to witness in your heart and challenge you when you are doing something wrong. When you give your heart to Christ, he will make it uncomfortable for you to sin and tell you inside of you when you are doing something wrong.

When God gave Abraham the covenant, he gave it to him in Christ. So, the Law, the Mosaic Law, and Covenant, which came 430 years later, cannot cancel what God had already given to Abraham before Moses came. If the inheritance was based on the Law, it would not be a promise from God, but God gave it to Abraham through a promise. Now, in Hebrews 8, the Lord is saying that the purpose of the Law was to show the transgression until the Seed, Christ, came. When he came, the Law became unnecessary because God is now the witness in our hearts to His Law. He will witness in our hearts and challenge us when we do wrong. We can't blame Moses, Aaron, the pastor, the evangelist, or the prophet anymore because God has created a witness in our hearts.

"Why then was the Law given at all? It was given alongside the promise to show people their sins. ***But the law was designed to last only until the coming of the "Seed" the child who was promised.*** *When God gave the law, he gave it first to angels, they gave it to Moses, his mediator, who then gave it to the people."* (**Galatians 3:19 TPT**).

Why then was the Law given at all? It was given alongside the promise to show people their sins.

Now, what is the promise? It is the Abrahamic promise. Also, the law was designed to last only until the coming of the Seed-The Child who was promised.

Who was he promised to? To Abraham.

When God gave the Law, He gave it first to Angel, then to Moses his mediator, who then gave it to the people.

The Lord wrote his laws. Gave it to angels. Angels gave it to Moses. Moses gave it to the people. **But that was a stop-gap measure** until the Seed came. When the Seed came, it became what you call the New Covenant. It is new because of the method of operation. Even those that are beneficiaries are now different. They are no longer the biological children of Abraham alone anymore. It is now everyone that comes in through Christ.

So, when we open our Bibles and we begin to read the old, what we call the Old Testament (Genesis to Malachi), we must do so from context. When we understand it from context, we begin to realize what is still active today.

The New Covenant is based on better promises.

"But now He has obtained a more excellent ministry, inasmuch as He is also Mediator of a better covenant, which was established on better promises" (Hebrews 8:6). The promises were what was given originally to Abraham, of which Jesus now brought into fulfillment.

Why is it on better promises? It is because the curse has been broken.

*"And to the man he said, "Since you listened to your wife and ate from the tree whose fruit, I commanded you not to eat, the ground is cursed because of you. All your life you will struggle to scratch a living from it. It will grow thorns and thistles for you, though you will eat of its grains. By the sweat of your brow will you have food to eat until you return to the ground from which you were made. For you were made from dust, and to dust you will return." (**Genesis 3:17-19 NLT**).*

God cursed the earth or the ground that is for Adam and his descendants. *"And to the man he said, since you listened to your wife and ate from the tree whose fruit, I commanded you not to eat, the ground is cursed because of you."*

It was a ground that was cursed not Adam. So, the curse Adam was dealing with was the curse of the ground not the one on him per se in that context. However, when you go to the Mosaic Law, many of it was, if you do this, you'll be blessed, if you do that you be cursed.

When you read Deuteronomy 28 from verse 15, you begin to see the curses that were mentioned. What Jesus came to do based on better promises, is the fact that he broke the curse of the law.

God is saying that because you are in Christ, the blessing of Abraham becomes your portion. As long as you obey God through Christ, the blessing of God is your portion. The curse can't work on you anymore.

*Yet, Christ paid the full price to set us free from the curse of the law. He absorbed the curse completely as he became a curse in our place. For it is written: "Everyone who is hung upon a tree is cursed." Jesus Christ dissolved the curse from our lives, so that in him all the blessings of Abraham can be poured out upon gentiles. And now through faith we receive the promised Holy Spirit who lives in us. (**Galatians 3:13-14 TPT**).*

Now, where did the Law come from? Moses. The curse didn't come from Adam. It came from Moses, and it was the curse of disobedience. That is why living in disobedience is a dangerous thing for believers. Another reason it is a better promise is that the Holy Spirit has been given to us. He is the Spirit of truth. Jesus said, "The Spirit will guide us into all truth." (John 16:13) We don't need Moses or Aaron any longer to guide us again. We are in a better covenant.

There is absolutely nothing you need for life the covenant did not cover.

Prayer

Say with me

My Father Jehovah Yahweh, I come to you because I am in Christ, and I am in the new covenant. All the blessings of Abraham are mine and I receive them right now in the name of Jesus. I am your firstborn. I am the new Israel, anything touching your firstborn, you will touch it as well in the name of Jesus.

CHAPTER FOUR

YOUR GLORIOUS NEW COVENANT

"For if that first covenant had been faultless, then no place would have been sought for a second... In that He says, "A new covenant," He has made the first obsolete. Now what is becoming obsolete and growing old is ready to vanish away." (Hebrews 8:7,13)

The Principles for Comparison

There cannot be a new covenant if there is no old one. The concept of new shows there is an old. What is the Old Covenant? If you do not know, go back to the previous chapter and study again. The Mosaic covenant is the old covenant and in some biblical references, it is called the first covenant. It is the covenant that was abolished to make way for the new covenant in Christ Jesus.

Paul's writing to the church in Corinth provides some basis for comparison between the old or first covenant and the new covenant. We take a look at 2 Corinthians 3:

We have such trust through Christ toward God. Not that we are sufficient of ourselves to think of anything as being from ourselves, but our sufficiency is from God, who also made us sufficient as ministers of the new covenant, not of the letter but of the spirit ***(2 Corinthians 3:4-6).***

This new covenant is a covenant of the Spirit. The old one is that of letters, and Bible says it is a killer. It administers death.

See from verse 7:

*"**But if the ministry of death, which is the Old Covenant** written and engraved on stones, was glorious, **so that the children of Israel could not look steadily at the face of Moses** because of the glory of his countenance, which glory was passing away."*

This also confirms it's the Mosaic Covenant. We see reference to the law that was written and engraved on stones, and the face of Moses (Read Exodus 34) that shone so brightly that the people could not look at his face. As brilliant as this is, it is the glory that is fading away.

Reading on:

*"How will the ministry of the Spirit not be more glorious? For if the ministry of condemnation had glory, the ministry of righteousness exceeds much more in glory. For even what was made glorious had no glory in this respect, because of the glory that excels. For if what if is passing away was glorious, what remains is much more glorious. Therefore, since we have such hope, we use great boldness of speech- unlike Moses, who put a veil over his face so that the children of Israel could not look steadily at the end of what was passing away. But their minds were blinded. For until this day the same veil remains unlifted in the reading of the Old Testament, because the veil is taken away in Christ. But even to this day, when Moses is read, a veil lies on their heart. Nevertheless, when one turns to the Lord, the veil is taken away." (**vv8-16**)*

Old Covenant	**New Covenant**
Covenant of the letter	Covenant of the Spirit
Ministry of death	Ministry of life
Fading glory	Glory that Excels (More Glorious)

Ministry of Condemnation	Ministry of Righteousness
Passing away	Remains
Veil exists (Minds blinded)	No Veil (Removed in Christ)

Now when we examine this scripture, we see that what was given to Moses was temporary. It was going to fade away and, as the scripture says, 'it kills.' However, despite this, there was glory on Moses' face, and he was radiant because of the glory of the Lord upon him. This glory was not necessarily there to give life to the people listening to him, but the people of Israel could not look at his face because their hearts couldn't take it.

So, they had to put a veil on his face before he could speak to the people. This veil still remains in their hearts because they can't see the purpose of God behind the law. The veil is still there when Moses is being read. Apostle Paul is telling us that if the temporary things given to Moses were glorious, how much more glorious is the thing that can give life?

Do you see the point he's making here? The scripture says that this veil is taken away when we find ourselves in Christ. We might think that when we are in Christ, everything is finished, and the veil is taken away so we can see what is even more glorious. But the Bible says that as we behold Him in verse 18.

*"But we all, with unveiled face, beholding as in a mirror the glory of the Lord, are being transformed into the same image from glory to glory, just as by the Spirit of the Lord." (**v18**)*

So, the glory you see today should not be the same glory you see tomorrow. The dimension of glory you walk in today should not be the same dimension of glory you walk in tomorrow. We are going from glory to glory.

Reading verse 18 from the Amplified Version of the Bible makes this point even clearer.

"And we all, with unveiled face, continually seeing as in a mirror the glory of the Lord, are progressively being transformed into His image from [one degree of] glory to [even more] glory, which comes from the Lord, [who is] the Spirit." (v18 AMP)

Hello reader, can you pause and imagine what the glory of the Lord is? What is the manifestation of the glory of the Lord? A manifestation of the glory of the Lord in the days of Moses was the various things that God did through him. *The Bible says that the law came through Moses, but grace and truth came through Jesus Christ* ***(John 1:17).***

When Jesus came, he was the embodiment of the glory of God in his day, and then he started doing His own signs, miracles and things which were far greater than what Moses could ever do.

In the days of Jesus, demons could be cast out but in the days of Moses, that could not happen. In the days of, Jesus, you can open the eyes of the blind but in the days of Moses, you can't necessarily open the eyes of the blind. In the days of Jesus, you could set somebody free, who is demonized, but in the days of Moses, you can't set somebody free, who was demonized.

There was a glory that was present in the time of Jesus that did not exist in the time of the Old Covenant. And the glory that we are seeing in Jesus is much more than the glory that ever existed in Moses. I hear many people saying; these are the days of Elijah. No! It is not. These are the days of Jesus. There is a greater glory when we compare both days when we use Moses and Elijah as our yardstick, I am not saying we can't use them as examples, but what I'm saying is if they become the yardstick, we are linking with the glory that is fading away or the glory that is dead.

Hebrews 11 in the Bible shows us that even though it lists all of those who are known for their faith, it goes on to say that they did not receive the fulfillment of the promise because they were waiting for the true glory to come, which is Jesus Christ. All of these people had faith, but they could not fully receive what was promised to them until Jesus arrived.

*"And all these, having obtained a good testimony through faith, did not receive the promise, God having provided something better for us, that they should not be made perfect apart from us." (**Hebrews 11:39-40**)*

There is a difference between the old and the new glory. The current glory is the best of all glories. In order to understand this, I have created a list of comparisons between the old and the new glory, or rather, the old and new covenants separate from the list you have seen tabulated earlier in this chapter. It is important to keep in mind a few principles when making these comparisons. These principles include:

The Principle of Justification

When discussing the old covenant and the new covenant, we will address the first principle of justification. Justification is the declaration of a person to be just or righteous. It is a legal term signifying acquittal. In the old covenant, it was not possible to be justified. Paul wrote to the Galatians saying: "no one is justified by the law in the sight of God". However, in the new covenant, it is guaranteed that one can be justified.

*For as many as are of the works of the law are under the curse; for it is written, "Cursed is everyone who does not continue in all things which are written in the book of the law, to do them." But that no one is justified by the law in the sight of God. For the just shall live by faith" (**Galatians 3:10 -11**).*

Principle of Life

The old covenant could not give life, but the New Covenant does.

Is the law then against the promises of God? Certainly not! God forbid: For if there had been a law given which could have given life, truly righteousness would have been by the law ***(Galatians 3:21).***

Here, we're talking about being born again and the concept of life. In the old covenant, it was not possible to be "born again" or to have new life. But in the new covenant, it is possible because of the power of the Spirit of God. Not only does the Spirit give new life to our spirits, but it also has the power to quicken, or make new, our mortal bodies. This is something to be celebrated and give thanks for. Hallelujah!

It is amazing to see the transformation that can take place in someone's life when they give their heart to the Lord. Sometimes, people who were previously trapped in destructive behaviors like drugs or alcohol are able to turn their lives around and find peace and joy in their relationship with God. This transformation is not just limited to the spiritual realm but can also be seen in the physical body. When someone has received the gift of new life through the Spirit of God, it can manifest in their appearance and demeanor. This is a powerful reminder of the life-giving power of the Spirit. It is not necessary to rely on prophets or other intermediaries to access this power. Instead, we can speak directly to any part of our bodies that may be in need of healing and life, and trust that the Spirit will work to bring healing and new life and you can base your faith on Romans 8:11.

"But if the Spirit of Him who raised Jesus from the dead dwells in you, He who raised Christ from the dead will also give life to your mortal bodies through His Spirit who dwells in you." (**Romans 8:11**)

Principle of Sin and Righteousness

The role of the old covenant was to reveal sin. It assigned sin and said, "This is what sin looks like." For those in the old covenant, there was a revelation of sin. Paul was speaking in Romans 6 and continued in Romans 7, and he said that before the law came, he considered himself a good person. However, once the law came, it revealed the sin that was already in him.

The role of the old covenant is to reveal sin and the role of the new covenant is to reveal righteousness. If you go to a place and every time, all they talk about is sin, they are walking in the old covenant. You are not supposed to be reminded of sin all the time, but righteousness.

"For the law, having a shadow of the good things to come and not the very image of the things, can never with these same sacrifices, which they offer continually year by year, make those who approach perfect. For then would they not have ceased to be offered? For the worshippers, once purified, would have had no more consciousness of sins. But in those sacrifices, there is a reminder. For it is not possible that the blood of bulls and goats could take away sin ***(Hebrews 10:1-4).***

Every year, there is a remembrance of sin. People are required to bring their offerings as a way of acknowledging their sinfulness. It doesn't matter whether or not a person's family has sinned that year, they are still required to bring their offerings because it is a revelation of sin. This practice helps to remind people of their sinfulness and the need for atonement.

Yes, the righteousness of God was revealed through the New Covenant, which was established through the death and resurrection of Jesus Christ. Through faith in Jesus, believers are made righteous in God's sight and are empowered to live a righteous life through the indwelling of the Holy Spirit. In Romans 3:21-22, the Bible says *"But now the righteousness of God apart from the law is revealed, being witnessed by the Law and the Prophets, even the righteousness of God, through faith in Jesus Christ, to all and on all who believe. For there is no difference."* In other words, through Jesus, we can receive the righteousness of God as a gift, rather than trying to earn it through our own efforts or through following the laws of the Old Testament. This righteousness gives us the power to live a holy and obedient life, pleasing to God.

Principle of Freedom.

The fourth principle is the principle of freedom. The old covenant led to bondage, as it was impossible to keep all the terms of the old covenant. However, in the New Covenant, there is freedom. Freedom is in the new covenant in which we are in right now, not the old covenant. The old covenant kept people in bondage, but a new covenant made you free in Christ.

Even so we, when we were children, were in bondage under the elements of the world. But when the fullness of the time had come, God sent forth His Son, born of a woman, born under the law, that we might receive the adoption as sons ***(Galatians 4:3).***

"But whenever a person turns [in repentance and faith] to the Lord, the veil is taken away. Now the Lord is the Spirit, and where the Spirit of the Lord is, there is liberty [emancipation from bondage, true freedom]." (2 Corinthians 3:16-17 AMP)

So, in a nutshell, he moved away from slavery to sonship, from bondage to freedom, and that is what the New Covenant did for you.

Principle of Transformation.

In the old covenant, there was no transformation from within. It was all about what you do externally but in the New Covenant, there is a transformation from within.

What the Lord does in the new covenant by His Spirit is transforming us from within. This is a present-continuous tense. He says, *"I will put my law in their minds and write it on their heart, I will be their God and they shall be my people."* By this, there is a transformation from within. So that our outside will reflect what is happening inside. So, the manifestation outside will be a fruit of what is happening inside.

I have used this illustration for many people to help them understand that when you see someone acting a certain way, their actions are revealing what is happening inside of them. The outside reflects the inside. The New Covenant is cut to fix what is within us so that we can manifest proper behavior on the outside.

I will put my law in their minds and write it on their heart, I will be their God and they shall be my people. No more shall every man teach his neighbor and every man his brother, saying, 'Know the Lord; forever say no to the Lord for they will all do what? Know me ***(Jeremiah 31: 34).***

Do you have a brother, sister, child, relative, or a neighbor that is all messed up? You can go to God and say, Lord, fix them from the inside because that is what God will do.

The Principle of the Curse and the Blessing

In the Old Covenant, God said, 'If you do this, then I will do that. If you do not do this, then this will come upon you. There were consequences for disobedience, as seen in Deuteronomy 28.

However, in the New Covenant, Jesus took away the curse of the law and left us with a requirement for consistent obedience. If you claim to be a child of God, you must live a life of consistent obedience to Jesus. Galatians 3 states that Christ redeemed us from the curse of the law by becoming a curse for us. He did this so that the blessings of Abraham might come upon the Gentiles.

"Christ purchased our freedom and redeemed us from the curse of the Law and its condemnation by becoming a curse for us—for it is written, "Cursed is everyone who hangs [crucified] on a tree (cross)"— in order that in Christ Jesus the blessing of Abraham might also come to the Gentiles, so that we would all receive [the realization of] the promise of the [Holy] Spirit through faith." (***Galatians 3:13-14 AMP***)

Keep this in mind as you strive to live out your faith. You are no longer under the curse for you have been redeemed from it. The blessing of Abraham is on you as long as you are in Christ.

Principle of Atonement and Remission

In the Old Covenant, atonement was used to cover sins rather than remove them. The blood of bulls and goats did not actually remove the sin, but rather covered it. It was like putting a clean cloak on a dirty person or using cologne to cover up a lack of personal hygiene. This is what atonement looked like in the Old Covenant. God covered the sin so that He didn't have to see it, but the sin remained. In contrast, in the New Covenant, Jesus' sacrifice actually removes our sins and reconciles us with God.

"For the law, having a shadow of the good things to come, and not the very image of the things, can never with these same sacrifices, which they offer continually year by year, make those who approach perfect. For then would they not have ceased to be offered? For the worshipers, once purified, would have had no more consciousness of sins. But in those sacrifices, there is a reminder of sins every year. ***For it is not possible that the blood of bulls and goats could take away sins."*** (**Hebrews 10:1-4**)

"But this Man, after He had offered one sacrifice for sins forever, sat down at the right hand of God... For by one offering He has perfected forever those who are being sanctified." (**Hebrews 10:12,14**)

In the Old Testament, atonement was used to cover sins. As it is written, it is impossible for the blood of bulls and goats to take away sin. But in the New Covenant, there is remission of sins. According to Kenneth Hagin Ministries explaining "Remission", if a cleaning agent is applied to an ink stain, the stain remover eradicates the ink. The stain wouldn't have to be covered over, because it would be cleansed, or erased. This is a picture of the remission of sins. When we receive Christ as our Savior, we become new creatures in Him (2 Cor. 5:17). Everything we've done in our past, and everything we've been, is wiped out. In God's eyes, it no longer exists. We begin again with a clean slate.

Remission means "a wiping out as though it had never been."

This means that when we sin, the Lord forgives us and wipes away our sins, remembering them no more. When Jesus made the new covenant, He promised to forgive our sins and transgressions and to remember them no more. This means that once we accept Christ, all of our past sins are wiped away and forgotten by God. Even if we try to remind God of a sin we committed in the past, He may respond by saying, 'I can't remember, what exactly did you do?

Some people keep track of all the wrongs someone else has done and only forgive them if they ask for forgiveness but never forget the wrong. But God is not like that in the New Covenant. When we accept Jesus as our Lord and Savior and ask for forgiveness, He wipes away all of our sins, including those committed since we were born. The blood of Christ allows for the remission of our sins. In contrast, Karma is the belief that there are consequences for our actions in this life or in future life. In Christ, we are forgiven, and our slate is wiped clean.

The difference is significant. In the old covenant, God promised to atone for people's sins, but they kept committing new ones and it was like putting a new, clean cloth on a dirty one. God eventually said he couldn't continue this way and made a new covenant. Under this new covenant, people will still sin, but God will wipe away their sin through the blood of his son, Jesus, and will not even remember it anymore. The devil may try to remind people of their past sins, but they can respond by pointing to the blood that was shed on the cross as payment for their sins.

"For He made Him who knew no sin to be sin for us, that we might become the righteousness of God in Him." (**2 Corinthians 5:21**)

Jesus, who knew no sin, became sin itself on the cross. He willingly took on all of humanity's sins and paid the price for it. He descended into hell and three days later, he rose from the dead and ascended to heaven, taking the keys of death and Hades with him. Now, the devil does not have the power to hold us captive. This is the significance of the new covenant. If we truly understand what Jesus did for us and the ~~cost~~ price he paid, we will be motivated to follow him and serve him with all our hearts. Even though we will never fully understand the cost of our salvation on this side of heaven, we can be grateful and devoted to Jesus for what he has done for us.

The Principle of Priesthood

In the old covenant, the priesthood was based on the lineage of Aaron and the tribe of Levi. However, the new priest, Jesus, came from the tribe of Judah, and his priesthood was based on the order of Melchizedek.

"And having been perfected, He became the author of eternal salvation to all who obey Him, called by God as High Priest "according to the order of Melchizedek," of whom we have much to say, and hard to explain, since you have become dull of hearing." (**Hebrews 5:9-11**)

This meant that his priesthood had no beginning and no end, unlike the Aaronic and Levitical priesthoods. Jesus' priesthood was eternal and unchanging, and he was able to enter the Most Holy Place once and for all, offering the perfect sacrifice for the sins of humanity.

*"For such a High Priest was fitting for us, who is holy, harmless, undefiled, separate from sinners, and has become higher than the heavens, who does not need daily, as those high priests, to offer up sacrifices, first for His own sins and then for the people's, for this He did once for all when He offered up Himself. For the law appoints as high priests men who have weakness, but the word of the oath, which came after the law, appoints the Son who has been perfected forever." (**Hebrews 7:26-28**)*

This marked a significant change from the old covenant, in which the priests had to offer sacrifices on a regular basis for the forgiveness of sins.

The Principle of Fellowship

The principle of fellowship states that the old covenant did not bring people close to God. The people stayed in the outer court, while the priest remained in the inner court. Only the high priest could enter the holy of holies, where the mercy seat and cherubim were located. The Lord sat upon the mercy seat, as he was above it. The high priest entered the holy of holies once a year, being careful not to make any mistakes. A rope was tied on him in case he was unable to come out, as no one could enter to bring him out. This shows the importance and holiness of the mercy seat and the presence of God within it

The old covenant was not one of intimacy, fellowship, or close connection with God. But when Jesus launched the new covenant, he declared that it was finished on the cross and gave up his spirit. The curtains of the holy of holies were torn in two, signifying that the place was now wide open for everyone to enter. We can now approach the throne of grace boldly, coming before our Father and God because someone has paid the price for us.

"Therefore, brethren, having boldness to enter the Holiest by the blood of Jesus, by a new and living way which He consecrated for us, through the veil, that is, His flesh, and having a High Priest over the house of God, let us draw near with a true heart in full assurance of faith, having our hearts sprinkled from an evil conscience and our bodies washed with pure water." (**Hebrews 10:19-22**)

Under the old covenant, we would have had to queue up and offer sacrifices of goats and lambs to a priest. But thanks to the new covenant, we can approach God directly, offering praise and thanksgiving to Him.

Principle of Dominion

The principle of dominion in the old covenant was only for one nation and one people, specifically the descendants of Jacob and the nation of Israel and their slaves. However, with the new covenant, the promise of Abraham was fulfilled, and all nations of the earth were blessed. This means that the covenant is no longer limited to a specific group of people but is open to all nations. It doesn't matter what your skin color is, the texture of your hair, your height, your weight, or what language you speak. Everyone has the opportunity to come to the master as one, with no distinctions between free or bound, Jew or Gentile. This is the fulfillment of the new covenant.

"For as many of you as were baptized into Christ have put on Christ. There is neither Jew nor Greek, there is neither slave nor free, there is neither male nor female; for you are all one in Christ Jesus. And if you are Christ's, then you are Abraham's seed, and heirs according to the promise." (**Galatians 3:27-29**)

It is indeed a glorious time that we are living in, as we have access to the new covenant and all of its blessings through Jesus. The Holy Spirit breaks out in a powerful way in our lives, even more so than in the days of Moses. We have the opportunity to approach the Father anytime, not just once a year or once a month, but every moment of every day. Through the spirit of adoption, we can cry out "Abba Father" and experience His presence in a personal and intimate way.

This is truly a blessing that should be celebrated and appreciated.

CHAPTER FIVE

KNOW YOUR COVENANT

And he said, Lord GOD, whereby shall I know that I shall inherit it? ***(Genesis 15:8).***

The keyword in the opening Scriptural text is "KNOW." The Lord spoke to Abraham in a vision and told him not to be afraid, assuring him that He is his shield. Abraham responded by questioning how he will have descendants, as he is childless, and his only (supposed) heir is his servant Eliezer. The Lord tells Abraham that Eliezer will not be his heir, but rather a descendant from his own body. The Lord then takes Abraham outside and tells him to look up at the stars and count them if he can, saying that his descendants will be as numerous as the stars.

From a human perspective, it may seem that Abraham was in doubt by his question (Genesis 15:8) "*Lord GOD, whereby shall I know that I shall inherit it*?" even after the LORD has spoken to him? That is not the case. It was not a case of doubt but of clarity. The point Abraham was making was not about the ability of God or the authenticity of what God can do. His statement was based on the fact that he wanted to know the details of how this would happen. It wasn't a question about the nature of God or whether God could fulfill what he said, it was a question of, "I want to know the details of what will happen. I want to know how it will happen.

There is nothing wrong with asking God for the details of the covenant He is bringing you into. Abraham wanted to know the things that God had included in the package he had for him.

"Then He said to Abram: "Know certainly that your descendants will be strangers in a land that is not theirs, and will serve them, and they will afflict them four hundred years. And also, the nation whom they serve I will judge; afterward they shall come out with great possessions. Now as for you, you shall go to your fathers in peace; you shall be buried at a good old age. But in the fourth generation they shall return here, for the iniquity of the Amorites is not yet complete." (**Genesis 15:13-16**)

Did that happen later on? You may ask. Yes, it did happen. He would not have known this if he hadn't asked for the details. God told him that his descendants would go to a land or nation that is not theirs and serve them, afflicting them for 400 years. So, Abraham knew the timelines. He knew it wouldn't be in his time and age or even the time of Isaac or Jacob. The passage goes on to say, *"And also the nation whom they serve, I will judge, and after that, they shall come out with great possession."* **(v14)**

So, Abraham knows that his descendants will be rich. And as for himself, he will *"go to his fathers in peace, He knew he would be buried at a good old age."* There are so many details in this passage of scripture that reveal things that gave Abraham peace of mind, knowing when things will happen, how they will happen, the assurance that they will happen, the timeline, and how long he will live on earth. *He will live to a very old age* (verse 15). These are details that he needed to know, and God wants us to know the details of the covenant He has given us too because what you know is what you can claim. What you know is what you can appropriate. What you know is what you can pray for, and what you know determines your state of mind.

It is important to know the details of the Covenant. This will allow us to claim, appropriate, pray for, and determine our state of mind regarding all that God has given us. For example, if we know that we will start a new job on a specific date in the future, we can be reassured and not worried about where money will come from in the present. To fully understand and benefit from the details of our covenant, we need to study the Bible and learn more about the promises that God has made to us as His children.

The example of the covenant between Jonathan and David in 1 Samuel 18 shows us what it means to come into a covenant with another.

Jonathan and David made a covenant together, agreeing that what was Jonathan's would become David's and vice versa. When Jonathan died, David searched for any surviving children of Jonathan to fulfill the covenant he had made with him. He found Mephibosheth who was living in Ledobah at the time, and he fulfilled it.

The story of Mephibosheth meeting with David illustrates the importance of being aware of the covenants we are a part of and how we can claim the blessings promised through them. Mephibosheth was ignorant of the covenant and the covenant promises between his father and David who was the king. If he knew, his life would have been different and better.

In the Bible, covenants are often mentioned as a way for people to remind God of the promises He has made and to claim the blessings He has promised. It is important for us to understand and remember the covenants God has made with us so that we can claim the blessings He has for us.

We illustrate some biblical examples of people who had to remind God of His covenant promises in prayer to get their desired results:

Moses:

"Then Moses pleaded with the Lord his God, and said: "Lord, why does Your wrath burn hot against Your people whom You have brought out of the land of Egypt with great power and with a mighty hand? Why should the Egyptians speak, and say, 'He brought them out to harm them, to kill them in the mountains, and to consume them from the face of the earth'? Turn from Your fierce wrath and relent from this harm to Your people. Remember Abraham, Isaac, and Israel, Your servants, to whom You swore by Your own self, and said to them, 'I will multiply your descendants as the stars of heaven; and all this land that I have spoken of I give to your descendants, and they shall inherit it forever.'" (**Exodus 32:11-13**)

The children of Israel had messed up and created a golden calf (an idol) for themselves to which God was angry and would have destroyed them. Moses appealed to God based on the Abrahamic covenant and the covenant promises contained therein.

The next verse says:

"So the Lord relented from the harm which He said He would do to His people." (**v14**)

Imagine what you can do, achieve, and make happen as you engage God with His covenant and covenant promises. However, you must know your covenant promises.

Nehemiah:

"Remember, I pray, the word that You commanded Your servant Moses, saying, 'If you are unfaithful, I will scatter you among the nations; but if you return to Me, and keep My commandments and do them, though some of you were cast out to the farthest part of the heavens, yet I will gather them from there, and bring them to

the place which I have chosen as a dwelling for My name.'" (**Nehemiah 1:8-9**)

As the story goes, the children of Israel had messed up again and they were ruled by the Persians. It came to Nehemiah's attention that the walls of Jerusalem had broken down... and this prompted a passionate and heartfelt appeal to God for his people. In his prayer, Nehemiah had to remind God of the terms of His covenant which they have broken, and the aspect of restoration.

Beloved, invest your time in knowing your covenant and the promises contained in these covenants.

In the story from Luke chapter 13, Jesus heals a woman who has been afflicted with a spirit of infirmity for 18 years on the Sabbath. The ruler of the synagogue is indignant and tells Jesus that healing should be done on other days, but Jesus responds by pointing out that the woman, a daughter of Abraham, is entitled to be set free from her infirmity on the Sabbath because of the covenant she is a part of. Jesus also uses the covenant to shame the ruler of the synagogue and all of his adversaries, showing that the covenant is higher than the rules they are trying to protect.

This passage also highlights the importance of remembering that we are children of the covenant and entitled to the blessings that come with it. If the devil is trying to bind us in any way, we can remind him that we cannot be bound because of the covenant of Abraham. We can claim the blessings of the covenant in our finances, marriages, emotions, lives, and ministries. By claiming the blessings of the covenant, we can experience the freedom and joy that come from being in a relationship with God.

CHAPTER SIX

YOUR GOD BASED ON THE BLOOD COVENANT

"These all died in faith, not having received the promises, but having seen them afar off were assured of them, embraced them and confessed that they were strangers and pilgrims on the earth." (**Hebrews 11:13**)

Now, when we study the actions of God as a result of the blood covenant He made with Abraham and the patriarchs, we can understand what they experienced and have a better appreciation for the provisions of our own - the superior covenant. Scriptures says they saw it from afar off.

However, it is important to first understand what the covenant with Abraham entailed so that we can fully comprehend the additional benefits that we have received. In other words, we can understand that we have more than what they had by first understanding what they had.

Now let's go to Deuteronomy 7:9 *"Therefore know that the LORD your God, He is God, the faithful God who keeps covenant and mercy for a thousand generations with those who love Him and keep His commandments."*

Now, the question is: do you love Him? That has not changed. If you love Him and keep His commandments, then God will keep His covenant and show mercy for all time. When the Bible refers to "a thousand generations," it does not mean literally a thousand generations, but rather signifies the perpetual nature of God's covenant and His commitment to keeping it. In other words, His covenant and mercy are ongoing and eternal.

The conditions of the covenant have not changed either. In order to receive the blessings of the covenant, one must still love God and keep His commandments. These conditions must be met in order to receive the provisions and benefits of the covenant.

In Mark 12:29-31, Jesus is asked what the greatest commandment is, and he responds by saying, "... *And you shall love the Lord your God with all your heart and with all your soul and with all your mind and with all your strength. The second is this: 'You shall love your neighbor as yourself. There is no other commandment greater than these."*

The condition remains the same: you must love God. All things work together for those who love God. You must also continue to keep God's commandments.

A new commandment I give to you, that you love one another; as I have loved you, that you also love one another. By this all will know that you are My disciples if you have love for one another **(John 13:34-35).**

You cannot say that you don't love X or Y and expect the covenant to work for you. You must love them, even if you feel hate towards them. Love is what binds us, keeps us together, and drives us to fulfill the covenant. The Bible says that faith works through love. Without love, we negate the manifestation of the blood covenant in our lives.

Going back to the children of Israel, we see the original covenant that God made with Abraham, which we are also a part of.

And I will establish My covenant between Me and you and your descendants after you in their generations, for an everlasting covenant, to be God to you and your descendants after you **(Genesis 17:7)**.

In the New Covenant, we see that God establishes His covenant with us and our descendants as an everlasting covenant. This is mentioned in Galatians 3, where it says that we, as believers in Christ, are Abraham's seed and are part of this covenant. God also tells us the basis of this covenant, saying that He will be God to us and our descendants.

It's important to understand the practical implications of God being our God. He is taking on the responsibility of being our God and guiding us in our lives. This means that He will provide for us, protect us, and be present with us. It's a covenant of relationship and reliance on God for all of our needs.

When God says that He will be God over us and our descendants, He is saying that He will be responsible for every aspect of our lives. He will guide us, give us assignments to fulfill and provide for us. He is saying that nothing else will take His place in our lives because He has chosen to be our God. As our God, He will be our provider, our deliverer, our healer, and our physician. Even if we don't appreciate His provision or have a bad attitude, He will still provide for us because He is our loving Father in this covenant relationship.

I will be the answer to your needs and prayers. I will be the solution to the problems that you have because I chose to be God over you.' So, when God says, 'I am God,' He is saying clearly that no matter what your needs are, if I have to create it, I will do it. If it does not exist, I will make it exist. I will take the hearts of men and turn them in your favor. I will show those who have asked what can become of you that because I am God over here, I will elevate you in their midst because of the covenant.

*"He also brought them out with silver and gold, and there was none feeble among His tribes. Egypt was glad when they departed, for the fear of them had fallen upon them. He spread a cloud for a covering, and fire to give light in the night. The people asked, and He brought quail, and satisfied them with the bread of heaven. He opened the rock, and water gushed out; it ran in the dry places like a river. For He remembered His holy promise, and Abraham His servant. He brought out His people with joy, His chosen ones with gladness. He gave them the lands of the Gentiles, and they inherited the labor of the nations, that they might observe His statutes and keep His laws. Praise the Lord!" (**Psalm 105:37-45**)*

Due to the covenant, he had made with Abraham, God ensured that the Israelites did not leave empty-handed. They were given silver and gold, and none of them were weak or sick. They were able to walk through the wilderness for 40 years without any illness because of the covenant God had made with Abraham. God provided everything they asked for because of this covenant.

Now, if those who had an inferior covenant will enjoy the blessings of the Lord in that dimension, how much more will we, with a better covenant, enjoy these blessings if we trust in him? God will be our Jehovah Rapha, taking sickness and disease away from us. He is telling the children of Israel, "I am your holy physician; you don't need medication.

I am not telling you not to take medication. If you are on medication please do not stop because I said so, but make sure you have the faith if you're going in that direction. The Lord has said in His Word, I am your physician; I am your Rapha, I am the one that will heal you, I am the one that will fix you.

It is worth considering that in the wilderness, where there were no doctors or nurses, the Israelites were still able to deliver babies and receive healing from God. This demonstrates the power of faith and the importance of understanding the revelation of God's healing power. When we have a deeper understanding and revelation of God's ability to sustain and provide for us, it can increase our faith and allow us to walk more closely with Him. Our level of revelation has a significant impact on how we experience God's blessings in our lives.

Through the blood covenant, God also becomes our *Jehovah Ezrah*-our helper. This means that no matter what area of life we need help in, God is obligated to assist us as His children. He will provide peace and protection for us, just as He did for the children of Israel when they were threatened by the superpower of Egypt. We can trust in God's faithfulness and His promise to help us as we navigate life's challenges.

The Amalek and the Philistines both tried and failed to conquer the children of Israel. My wife and I once read scripture about how Samuel built an altar called Ebenezer. He did this because the children of Israel had no weapons at all, not even enough men to fight when the Philistines were coming. They turned to Samuel and begged for his help, so he took an animal and offered a sacrifice to petition the Lord for their protection.

"Then Samuel took a stone and set it up between Mizpah and Shen, and called its name Ebenezer, saying, "Thus far the Lord has helped us." So the Philistines were subdued, and they did not come anymore into the territory of Israel. And the hand of the Lord was against the Philistines all the days of Samuel." (**1 Samuel 7:12-13**)

The Bible says that the Lord fought for the children of Israel from heaven against the Philistines. Despite being a small nation, Israel was able to defeat its enemies because God was on their side. The story of the war in Israel, against Egypt and other Arab nations, illustrates this point. When the Egyptian and other armies arrived to fight Israel, they saw the Israelite warriors and knew that they could not defeat them. They fled, and when the Israelites arrived at the battlefield, they saw what the enemies had seen: God's angels fighting for them. Despite being a small nation compared to powerful Egypt in the 6-day war, Israel was able to emerge victorious because of the blood covenant with God.

There is a story about a missionary who went to a village where the tribes were planning to kill him and his family because they were considered barbarians. As the tribesmen approached the missionary's location, they suddenly stopped and were unable to move for about 45 minutes. Eventually, they turned back and left. A few years later after this incidence, the chief of the village converted to Christianity. Now the missionary asked him, 'That day you came with the tribe to kill us, what happened?' The chief replied, 'Where did you get those men who stood in front of your hut? They were big, mighty warriors with swords in their hands, and we knew we couldn't defeat them. So we turned back and ran away.

"You shall serve the Lord your God, and He will bless your bread and your water. And I will take sickness away from the midst of you." ***(Exodus 23:25-26)***

This is covenanted statement made to a covenanted people. This is what the blood covenant will make God do. The bread and water represent your provision. He has made a covenant promise of blessing over it. You can take God by His Word.

... and I will take away sickness from the midst of you.

You can confront sickness with this covenant promise anytime it shows its ugly face. And then He goes on to say in verse 26, *"no one will suffer miscarriage, or be barren in your land, I will fulfill the number of your days."*

Psalm 91 says, "with long life will I satisfy you'.

So, you know the right Word to use over sickness and diseases. The Lord said, *"with long life, I will satisfy you, and the number of your days I will fulfill."*

You've got to know the covenant and its terms. Do you know why? Because the devil needs to be told, otherwise he will encroach. God said, I will do it all because of the covenant.

You need a provider? You need to be protected? You need help? You need aid in any area? He said I am your God. Any harm is coming after you? Any gang up against you? He said I am your God because of the blood covenant.

When we celebrate the blood of Jesus that was shed on the cross at Calvary, let's do it with understanding and purpose, not just out of religious obligation. Jesus's blood was shed so that we might live our lives to the fullest. He came to give us life, and not just a manageable or pitiable life, but an abundant one. Let's allow Jesus to receive the glory for the great price he paid for us.

CHAPTER SEVEN

MERCY-BASED COVENANT

"To perform the mercy promised to our fathers and to remember His holy covenant, the oath which He swore to our father Abraham..." (Luke 1:72-73a)

Have you ever asked yourself why God would give man a covenant? Why was it given? One key possible answer is that it was given out of God's love for mankind, which is expressed through His mercy.

In Matthew chapter nine, Jesus saw a man named Matthew sitting at the tax office and tells him to follow him. Matthew gets up and follows Him. Later, as Jesus is sitting at a table in a house, many tax collectors and sinners come and sat with Him and His disciples. When the Pharisees saw this, they questioned Jesus' disciples. They asked, *"why is your master eating with tax collectors and sinners."* Jesus heard them, and said to them, *"Those who are well have no need of a physician, but those who are sick. But go and learn what this means: 'I desire mercy and not sacrifice.' For I did not come to call the righteous, but sinners, to repentance."*

The focus of this verse is on Jesus' statement to the Pharisees: *"I desire mercy, and not sacrifice."* This is the very heart of the Father towards all sinners. He wants to show them His mercy. The revelation of this will humble us. It will deliver us from a judgmental and critical spirit. Jesus says that God relates to us from a place of mercy. Without His mercy, we are all doomed. We are all products of God's mercy, and it is this mercy that is keeping us.

When we look at the various covenants that God has made with humanity, we can see that they are expressions of His mercy.

Edenic Covenant

Looking at the very first covenant between God and man, the Edenic Covenant, it was a covenant that at the end of it, by the mercies of God, redemption is offered to man.

The Edenic covenant although, not specifically called a covenant in the Bible, refers to the covenant made between God and Adam in Genesis. The Edenic covenant was a conditional covenant, that is, there was a responsibility on both sides. Adam was responsible to obey, and God would bless him with life. If Adam disobeyed and ate of the tree of the knowledge of good and evil, death would be the result (Genesis 2:16–17). Adam's life was conditional on his obedience.

Adam disobeyed God and broke the terms of the Edenic covenant, receiving the punishment of death. He did not die immediately, but he and Eve inherited death, and then passed it on to all their offspring, and death continues to this day to be the wages of sin (Proverbs 10:16; Romans 6:23). This covenant is among the most significant covenants between man and God, along with the Abrahamic covenant (a covenant where God promised to bless Abraham and his descendants forever), the Mosaic covenant (a covenant which involved the delivery of God's Law to Moses), the Noahic covenant, and the Davidic covenant.

The Edenic covenant had a second part, which is often called the Covenant of Redemption. As God was informing Adam and Eve about the curses their sin had caused, He revealed a covenant in His curse upon the Serpent when He said: *"And I will put enmity between you and the woman, and between your seed and her Seed; He shall bruise your head, and you shall bruise His heel." (Genesis 3:15).* The promised Seed is Jesus who brought redemption to man.

Taking that a step further, God kills an animal to clothe Adam and Eve after they sinned. He also banishes them from the garden and prohibits them from eating from the Tree of Life (Genesis 3:21-24), because if they did, their fallen nature as humans would become permanent. This is an example of how God's covenants with humanity are an expression of His mercy. God chased man out of the garden. He placed cherubim to prevent the fallen man from the tree of life so he could redeem him later. This is all of God's mercy at work. It was His act of mercy to have chased man away from the garden.

THE NOAHIC COVENANT

The Noahic covenant is a covenant between God and man based on the promise made by God to the human race never again to destroy the world with a flood. The promise was made to "every living creature" on the earth. God's promise in the Noahic covenant is sealed with the sign of the rainbow (Genesis 9:8-17).

When we see a rainbow in the sky, we are reminded of Noah's covenant with God. It is a sign of God's promise to Noah that He will never again destroy humanity with a flood. No matter how much sin there is on Earth, God will not destroy it again with a flood because of His Covenant promise to Noah. This is based on His mercy.

THE ABRAHAMIC COVENANT

The Abrahamic Covenant is really the beginning of God's decision to reach into humanity and specifically save people for Himself. It comes in the form of a promise to Abraham. Abraham, who was the son of an idolater, did not know God. God takes the initiative with him, calls him into a relationship with Himself, and made some promises to Abraham. He promised Abraham that he was going to be a great nation, that he was going to be given land, a place to live, and that through Him, all nations of the earth will be blessed. We see the beginning of the Abrahamic Covenant in Genesis 12.

Later on, in Genesis 17, the promise is given a specific condition which is the requirement of circumcision. Abraham and his son, Ishmael, are circumcised, making clear that they and all of their household are set apart for the Lord. This covenant, this promise, of blessing to Abraham, to Abraham's seed, and then to the nations through Abraham really is the beginning of the covenant of grace that's going to find its fulfillment in Jesus Christ.

The Abrahamic covenant is also covenant based on mercy. God chose Abraham and told him to leave his people and go to a land that God would show him. Abraham did nothing for God to have chosen him. God wanted to extend mercy to mankind and create a model in which His blessings could be passed on to all people, not because of what they have done but because of who God is.

THE MOSAIC COVENANT AND THE DAVIDIC COVENANT

The Mosaic covenant and the Davidic covenant are also based on mercy. In the Davidic covenant, God says that He will keep His mercy with David forever (Psalm 89:28). He also says that David's seed will endure forever (v29), which refers to Jesus and His throne. The covenant with David will not be broken because it is based on mercy.

You can look at scriptures 2 Samuel 7:8-29, where the Davidic Covenant is discussed. This covenant is important because when Jesus is referred to as the "Son of David," it is in reference to the covenant mercy of God.

In Psalm 89:20, "*I have found My servant David; With My holy oil I have anointed him, with whom My hand shall be established; Also My arm shall strengthen him.*"

In verse 28, it says, "*My mercy I will keep for him forever, And My covenant shall stand firm with him.*"

Verse 29-37, talks about the seed of David, which refers to Jesus, enduring forever and his throne is established like the days of heaven.

However, it also mentions that if the sons of David, or natural children, do not follow the law, they will be punished. The covenant with David, however, stands and is based on mercy. This is important because even though some of the kings in the lineage of David were not perfect, the covenant with David and the promise of a savior through his line were upheld through God's mercy. Solomon was a classic example of a son in David's lineage who did not follow the Lord and sinned, yet God kept him on the throne and did not totally remove the kingdom from David's lineage because of His covenant and mercy.

"For it was so, when Solomon was old, that his wives turned his heart after other gods; and his heart was not loyal to the Lord his God, as was the heart of his father David. For Solomon went after Ashtoreth the goddess of the Sidonians, and after Milcom the abomination of the Ammonites. Solomon did evil in the sight of the Lord, and did not fully follow the Lord, as did his father David.... Therefore, the Lord said to Solomon, "Because you have done this, and have not kept My covenant and My statutes, which I have commanded you, I will surely tear the kingdom away from you and give it to your servant. Nevertheless, I will not do it in your days, <u>for the sake of your father David;</u> I will tear it out of the hand of your son. However, I will not tear away the whole kingdom; <u>I will give one</u>

tribe to your son for the sake of My servant David, and for the sake of Jerusalem which I have chosen."" (**1 Kings 11:4-6;11-13**)

The Bible records that God will keep this person on the throne because of their father David, due to the covenant based on mercy. When Jesus walked on earth, he had compassion, and it was this compassion that led people to be delivered and saved. The compassion of God brings us to the fullness of what God has for us and it is based on a covenant.

In Matthew 12:1-7, the Pharisees criticized Jesus' disciples for plucking heads of grain on the Sabbath, but Jesus pointed out that David and his companions ate the shewbread, which was only lawful for the priests to eat, and that the priests in the temple profaned the Sabbath but were blameless. Jesus then said, *"I desire mercy and not sacrifice,"* emphasizing the importance of mercy over following the letter of the law.

The mercy of the Lord awaits you by covenant. Through Jesus, the covenant promised the "Seed of Abraham" (Galatians 3:16) and the covenant promised the "Seed of David" (Romans 1:3), mercy awaits you. Everyone who hears and accepts the gospel has entered into a covenant relationship with God. Today, I ask you to accept Jesus as Lord and Savior if you have not.

When you say, 'Jesus, I receive you,' you should expect God the Father to forgive you and receive you as a son into His kingdom as if it were your right.

When we pray, we expect an answer as if it were our right. We approach God as if it were our right, but it is a right based on the covenant. We must realize that it is the mercy of God that allows us to approach Him in the first place, and it is the mercy of God that ensures that whatever we desire, we can receive as long as we walk according to His covenant.

Anyone living in condemnation should realize that mercy tells us we can't live in condemnation if we come to Jesus.

Paul reveals this in his letter to the church in Rome that there is no condemnation to anyone who is in Christ Jesus who do not walk according to the flesh, but according to the Spirit (Romans 8:1). The mercy of God as found in His new covenant with us reveals the heart of Father God.

Psalm 136 speaks of the covenant mercy of the Lord and through this covenant mercy, we see what God desires in plain view.

"Oh, give thanks to the Lord, for He is good! For His mercy endures forever. Oh, give thanks to the God of gods! For His mercy endures forever. Oh, give thanks to the Lord of lords! For His mercy endures forever: To Him who alone does great wonders, for His mercy endures forever; To Him who by wisdom made the heavens, for His mercy endures forever; To Him who laid out the earth above the waters, for His mercy endures forever; to Him who made great lights, for His mercy endures forever— The sun to rule by day, for His mercy endures forever; The moon and stars to rule by night, for His mercy endures forever. To Him who struck Egypt in their firstborn, for His mercy endures forever; and brought out Israel from among them, for His mercy endures forever; with a strong hand, and with an outstretched arm, for His mercy endures forever; to Him who divided the Red Sea in two, for His mercy endures forever; and made Israel pass through the midst of it, for His mercy endures forever; but overthrew Pharaoh and his army in the Red Sea, for His mercy endures forever; to Him who led His people through the wilderness, for His mercy endures forever; to Him who struck down great kings, for His mercy endures forever; and slew famous kings, for His mercy endures forever— Sihon king of the Amorites, for His mercy endures forever; and Og king of Bashan, for His mercy endures forever— And gave their land as a heritage, for His mercy

*endures forever; a heritage to Israel His servant, for His mercy endures forever. Who remembered us in our lowly state, for His mercy endures forever; and rescued us from our enemies, for His mercy endures forever; Who gives food to all flesh, for His mercy endures forever. Oh, give thanks to the God of heaven! For His mercy endures forever." (**Psalm 136**)*

The word "mercy" used in this psalm comes from the root word "*ḥeseḏ*": It indicates kindness, lovingkindness, mercy, goodness, faithfulness, love, and acts of kindness. This aspect of God is one of several important features of His character and what He extends toward mankind in covenants. The classic text for understanding the significance of this word is Psalm 136 where it is used twenty-six times to proclaim that God's kindness and love are eternal. The psalmist made it clear that God's kindness and faithfulness serve as the foundation for His actions and His character: it underlies His goodness (Ps. 136:1); it supports His unchallenged position as God and Lord (Ps. 136:2, 3); it is the basis for His great and wondrous acts in creation (Ps. 136:4-9) and delivering and redeeming His people from Pharaoh and the Red Sea (Ps. 136:10-15); the reason for His guidance in the desert (Ps. 136:16); His gift of the land to Israel and the defeat of their enemies (Ps. 136:17-22); His ancient, as well as His continuing deliverance of His people (Ps. 136:23-25); His rulership in heaven (Ps. 136:26). The entire span of creation to God's redemption, preservation, and the permanent establishment is touched upon in this psalm. It all happened, is happening, and will continue to happen because of the Lord's covenant faithfulness, mercy, and kindness.

The other more specific uses of the term develop the ideas contained in Psalm 136 in greater detail. Because of His mercy, He meets the needs of His creation by delivering them from enemies and despair (Gen. 19:19; Ex. 15:13; Ps. 109:26; Jer. 31:3); He preserves their lives and redeems them from sin (Ps. 51:1-3; 86:13). As Psalm 136 demonstrates, God's mercy is abundant, exceedingly great, without end, and good (Ex. 34:6; Num. 14:19; Ps. 103:8; 109:21; Jer. 33:11). He is the covenant-keeping God who maintains kindness and mercy (Deut. 7:9) to those who love Him.

It is the covenant mercy of God that kept the children of Israel and is keeping us. I'm not even going into the celestial things, like the sun, moon, and stars that God created. Do you know that the sun, moon, and stars, heavens were never made for God? God made all of these things for our benefit. He knew we would need the sun, moon, stars, and clouds.

When the children of Israel needed covenant mercy, God parted the Red Sea and delivered them. It was His covenant mercy that was working on their behalf. The same is true today. No matter what situation we find ourselves in, the covenant mercy of God can and will work for us. It is not just the forgiveness of sins (as crucial as that is), but it works in every area of our lives. It is mercy that will keep us standing, help us in all areas of life, and bless our children. When Jesus looked at the Pharisees and said, "go and learn what it means, I desire mercy," he was telling them that God relates to people from a place of mercy and that we should also walk in mercy.

CHAPTER EIGHT

THE COVENANT LOVE OF GOD

*"It is because of the Lord's loving-kindnesses that we are not consumed, because His [tender] compassions never fail. They are new every morning; Great and beyond measure is Your faithfulness." (**Lamentations 3:22-23 AMP**)*

God is love, and we know that His steadfast love never fails. God wants everyone to know that He is a loving God and Father forevermore.

*"Surely goodness and mercy and unfailing love shall follow me all the days of my life..." (**Psalm 23:6a AMP**)*

To the extent to which we grasp the revelation of God's love in general, and God's love for us is the extent to which we can appropriate all that God has for us in this life. It is possible that you trust God's power; you know His promises but, on the inside, you're wavering or doubting. You pray, but you are afraid to expect a miracle, a solution, an answer, etc. You are afraid of disappointment.

How can you be sure He'll come through for you? To answer that question, you need more than a knowledge of God's power and promises. You need a personal revelation of a covenant of love.

Covenant love is referred to in various terms in the Bible, but the main word used is "hesed". In fact, it is not a stretch to say that the word hesed in essence summarizes the entire history of God's covenantal relationship with Israel. *Hesed* is God's lovingkindness—the consistent, ever-faithful, relentless, constantly pursuing, lavish, extravagant, unrestrained, one-way love of God. It is often translated as covenant love, lovingkindness, mercy, steadfast love, loyal love, devotion, commitment, or reliability.

In Psalm 23, the real translation should be "surely goodness and *hesed* (or covenant love) shall follow me all the days of my life". This is the confidence that the Psalmist had in the covenant love of God.

That same love is declared in John 3:16...

*"For God so loved the world that He gave His only begotten Son, that whoever believes in Him should not perish but have everlasting life." (**John 3:16**)*

"For God so loved the world that He gave..." and He gave...and He gave...and He gave. That is the message the Bible brings us from the beginning to the end. It sounds simple enough. Yet few of us really comprehend it. This is the basis of God's covenant with mankind and the Bible is a story of God's love towards mankind through the generations.

God is itching to give... He just wants to lavish... He has you in mind to give you everything that pertains to life and godliness. THE BASIS OF THIS IS LOVE! Everlasting, unconditional, never-failing love - God's love; our natural minds cannot grasp it. Yet, Paul prayed in his letter to the Ephesians that we might *"... know the love of Christ which passes knowledge; that you may be filled with all the fullness of God." (**Eph. 3:19**).*

Why would Paul bow his knees petitioning God for these group of Christians at Ephesus? He knew how important it is that they "know" which is experiential knowledge – the love of Christ. This love is only known by experience (practically) and not by theoretical or theological ways.

The Message Translation puts it this way:

"And I ask him that with both feet planted firmly on love, you'll be able to take in with all followers of Jesus the extravagant dimensions of Christ's love. Reach out and experience the breadth! Test its length! Plumb the depths! Rise to the heights! Live full lives, full in the fullness of God." (**Ephesians 3:17-19 MSG**)

How can we comprehend the incomprehensible love? We can't! At least, not with simple human understanding. To know something as vast as the love of God requires a revelation given through the power of the Holy Spirit. Revelation is comprehension imparted into our spirit from the Holy Spirit and transmitted into our minds. It doesn't pass from the head to the heart. It must come from the heart to the head.

God wants to bring you into the depths of His love; the revelation of His love...that you might be filled or that you might receive that He is giving. The depth of your revelation of His love will translate to the level of your expectation to receive from God.

And may the grace of God reveal to us a love that goes beyond being just an academic or intellectual understanding, but rather a love that is experienced and felt deeply. A love that is so strong and undeniable that it prevents us from ever doubting God's motives, abilities, or willingness. This love is not based on the circumstances or events happening around us, but rather it is immeasurable and unconditional.

God's Love is immeasurable, and he loves you despite everything. His love for you is deep and passionate. He loves you more than you love yourself. When you go through pain or challenges, he goes through them with you. Just like when Saul was persecuting the church and Jesus appeared to him, saying "why are you persecuting me?" (Acts 9:4) When anything touches one of Jesus' disciples, it touches Jesus himself.

Surely, goodness, and mercy shall follow me, all the days of my life, and I will dwell in the house of the Lord, forever and ever **(Psalm 23:6).**

When the Psalmist says 'surely,' he is expressing confidence in the conclusion of his statement. He says 'surely' as a way of emphasizing that no matter the circumstances, he will not fear evil. This means that the time of day or the month of the year does not matter because he is sure of his belief in this God of love.

The Psalmist declared, goodness and mercy, which represent covenant love, will follow him. This is not a prayer, but rather a statement of truth and fact. It reflects the innermost beliefs and confessions of the speaker. The Psalmist has come to a revelation after examining everything in his life. He knows that no matter what stage of life he is in, or what time of day or year it is, one thing is certain: the goodness and mercy of God, represented by covenant love, will follow him wherever he goes. This is a deeply personal conviction for the Psalmist, and he is certain that the love of God will follow him throughout his life.

As believers in Christ, can we make the same confession as the Psalmist? Can we wake up every morning with the assurance that no matter what circumstances we face, the goodness and mercy of God, represented by covenant love, will follow us throughout our lives? This should be a source of confidence for us as believers, and it is something that we should bear in mind as we go through life.

Many of us have no problem believing in the power of God or knowing what His promises say. However, the issue of His will can sometimes be a disconnect for us. When we understand the covenant love of God, we know that it is love that motivates him. All of God's motivation is based on love because He is love (1 John 4:8). Everything he did with the children of Israel was based on love, even when they had to suffer the consequences of their disobedience. God's love for them was constant, and he always sought to bring them back to him. Sometimes, love may seem challenging, but it is still love. For example, when a parent sends their child to school, it may not be what the child wants at the time, but it is out of love for their future. The parent can see the benefits of an education and the future opportunities it can provide, while the child may only see the difficulties of learning certain subjects. Similarly, the challenges we face in life may not be easy, but they are happening for a reason and are taking us to where we are meant to be.

In John 3:16, The Bible says *"For God, so loved the world that he gave..."*

Now you can put your name to replace 'the world' because 'the world' is you at this present time. You were the reason Jesus went to the cross. You were the reason Jesus was beaten, and a crown of thorns was placed on Him. You were the reason He was crucified.

The Bible says that God so loved the world that he gave his only begotten son to suffer on the cross for our sake. This demonstrates the depth of God's love for us, even though we have a tendency to rebel against him. It is not a question of whether God loves us more than he loves His Son, but rather that the love of God is not partial and the price he was willing to pay to redeem us was the sacrifice of His only begotten Son. This should help us to understand the reasoning of love and the lengths to which God is willing to go for us. If you were the only one left in the whole world, he would have still done it for you.

Despite His deep love for the son, He was willing to send Him to the cross because of His love for us. The son, who was with God at the beginning and is himself, God, willingly laid down His life on the cross and took it up again. This demonstrates the motivation behind God's actions: love. He was willing to make the ultimate sacrifice for the people he loves.

In the natural, if we love someone and they refuse to reciprocate that love, it can be difficult to keep showing them love. However, God's love for us is unconditional and by covenant. It is a consistent, faithful, relentless, and extravagant love that is not dependent on receiving reciprocal love in return.

God's covenant with Abraham in Genesis 17 is based on love. God made up his mind to love Abraham and chose to embrace him, pouring out all of His love on him. When God sent His Son into the world, He did so out of love and not with the expectation of receiving anything in return. Love gives, and it requires action. God demonstrated his love for us through the action of sending His Son to the cross for our redemption. It is important for us to understand and enter into the revelation of God's love, so that we can operate from a place of being filled with his love.

As it says in Ephesians 3:19, we can be filled with the fullness of God's love.

"to know the love of Christ which passes knowledge; that you may be filled with all the fullness of God. Now to Him who is able to do exceedingly abundantly above all that we ask or think, according to the power that works in us, to Him be glory in the church by Christ Jesus to all generations, forever and ever. Amen ***(Ephesians 3:19-21).***

Paul is praying for the church in Ephesians 3 and asking that they may know the love of Christ, which surpasses knowledge. This means that we cannot fully understand or comprehend the love of God. Yes, we must seek a revelation of it through the Spirit of

God, who will open our hearts and pour in the love of God. When we truly understand and experience the love of God, it changes our entire perspective, and our lives are transformed.

What the Bible is telling us to do is that we embrace the totality of the revelation of the love of God. This will transform our lives.

GOD WANTS TO BRING YOU AND I INTO THE REVELATION OF HIS LOVE!

As I conclude this chapter, I will highlight four points to note as we learn from Jesus about the subject of love, the God who is love, and our covenants with God that are rooted in love.

1. ***Jesus Revealed the Basis of His Confidence in the Father – it is LOVE!***

"Then Jesus answered and said to them, "Most assuredly, I say to you, the Son can do nothing of Himself, but what He sees the Father do; for whatever He does, the Son also does in like manner. **For the Father loves the Son** *and shows Him all things that He Himself does; and He will show Him greater works than these, that you may marvel."* (**John 5:19-20**)

The Son can do nothing of Himself. The Father reveals and He (the Son) does the same. The miracles, signs, and wonders cannot stop because the Father loves the Son!!! Simple!

This also confirms that because Jesus is confident in the Love of the Father and grasps the revelation of love, He can keep receiving what the Father is showing, giving, releasing, etc. We ought to receive the revelation of the Father's love and let this revelation guide our hearts in our everyday life.

2. ***Jesus Revealed the Basis of His coming from the Father – It is LOVE!***

"For God so loved the world that He gave His only begotten Son, that whoever believes in Him should not perish but have everlasting life." (**John 3:16**)

The Love of God gave Jesus to us. The biggest, best, and most precious of gifts to mankind. It was love from the Father for Him to give us His only begotten son. This love from God for us should be the basis of our confidence in life. Paul wrote:

"What then shall we say to these things? If God is for us, who can be against us? He who did not spare His own Son, but delivered Him up for us all, how shall He not with Him also freely give us all things?" (**Romans 8:31-32**)

The confidence we have is this – if God the Father could not withhold Himself but was compelled by LOVE to give us Jesus – the best, biggest, etc., what will hinder God from giving us all things?

"But God demonstrates His own love toward us, in that while we were still sinners, Christ died for us. Much more then, having now been justified by His blood, we shall be saved from wrath through Him." (**Romans 5:8-9**)

Hope we get this. God demonstrated His own love toward us. It is in the past tense which means, it is already done. Christ died for us. Paul goes on to say, much more then... we shall be saved from wrath through Him.

3. ***Jesus Revealed that LOVE compelled Him to lay down His life for us***

This is no longer just the Father that was compelled by LOVE, but Jesus equally was compelled by LOVE to lay down His life.

"Greater love has no one than this, than to lay down one's life for his friends." (**John 5:13**)

Jesus called His disciples friends, even though some of them abandoned him when he was arrested, and one of them, Judas, betrayed him. Jesus demonstrated the greatest love by laying down his life for his friends. God is befriending us not because of who we are or what we have done, but because of what he can do in us and what we can become through him. We should not write ourselves off as not being friends of Jesus, even if we have not always walked with him in the way we should. God sees our potential and calls us friends in order to help us grow and become more like him.

Choose to embrace this love that Jesus is offering you and see your life transformed. You will have the capacity to love Jesus and love what and who He loves.

4. ***We have been instructed to be motivated by LOVE, to give ourselves...***

The covenant love of God that has been lavished on us is the basis from which we expect to receive from the Lord because He is a giver. He gives. However, this same covenant love is to compel us to also give – as an extension of God to mankind.

"By this we know love because He laid down His life for us. And we also ought to lay down our lives for the brethren." (**1 John 3:16**)

If the love of God fills us completely, it will be evident in the way we speak, act, and relate to others. We will love everyone, regardless of their appearance or circumstances, because the love of God flowing from within us is unconditional. When we are motivated by love, it will be the driving force in our lives and relationship:

- We are blessed by the covenant love of God.
- We receive because of the covenant love of God.

- We lack nothing because of the covenant love of God.
- We are responsible to others because we are recipients of the covenant love of God.
- We should let others know and bring them into this revelation of the covenant love of God.

CHAPTER NINE

KEEPING GOD'S COVENANT

"And God said to Abraham: "As for you, you shall keep My covenant, you, and your descendants after you throughout their generations. This is My covenant which you shall keep, between Me and you and your descendants after you: Every male child among you shall be circumcised; and you shall be circumcised in the flesh of your foreskins, and it shall be a sign of the covenant between Me and you. He who is eight days old among you shall be circumcised, every male child in your generations, he who is born in your house or bought with money from any foreigner who is not your descendant. He who is born in your house and he who is bought with your money must be circumcised, and My covenant shall be in your flesh for an everlasting covenant. And the uncircumcised male child, who is not circumcised in the flesh of his foreskin, that person shall be cut off from his people; he has broken My covenant. ***(Genesis 17:9-14).***

This scriptural passage reveals some very important factors with regards to covenant. It tells us that covenants can be kept or broken. This is a foundational truth that we all need to bear in mind. In the Book of Genesis, God preached the gospel to Abraham. God said to him, **"...in your seed shall all nations be blessed." (Galatians 3:8)** The scriptures say, *Abraham believed God and it was counted to him for righteousness. (**Genesis 15:6**)*

I want you to reconsider the text of these scriptures. God didn't say, Abraham, in your seed, Israel shall be blessed, rather he said, in your seed shall all nations be blessed. Abraham might not have understood what God was saying but God knew what He was saying because the seed as established in Galatians 3 was Christ. Christ is the seed that was spoken of, and it is through him that anyone can become a part of the Abrahamic covenant.

"Therefore, remember that you, once Gentiles in the flesh—who are called Uncircumcision by what is called the Circumcision made in the flesh by hands— that at that time you were without Christ, being aliens from the commonwealth of Israel and strangers from the covenants of promise, having no hope and without God in the world. But now in Christ Jesus you who once were far off have been brought near by the blood of Christ... Now, therefore, you are no longer strangers and foreigners, but fellow citizens with the saints and members of the household of God" (**Ephesians 2:11-13, 19**)

We can establish as well from Ephesians 2, that even when we were unbelievers and Gentiles, aliens from the commonwealth of Israel, and strangers from the covenants of promise, now through the blood of Jesus, we are partakers of the covenant and no longer strangers or aliens. We are now fellow citizens of the kingdom of Israel. We are part of that commonwealth.

Galatians 4:28 says, "*Now we, brethren, as Isaac was, are the children of promise.*"

We are the children of promise, just like Isaac was the child of promise. When God made that promise to Abraham, he had us in mind. In fact, you can look at yourself right now and say "when God was speaking to Abraham, He had me in mind. I am a child of promise, just like Isaac was. Hallelujah!

So, we know without a shadow of a doubt that we are the children of promise. Is that not amazing, just to even think about it, that we are the children of promise? We were promised ahead of time. It was pre-planned ahead of time that we would come, that we would exist, that we would be and every provision that was necessary for our life had already been taken care of because we were promised.

YOU DID NOT JUST SHOW UP

You were promised, you did not just show up. Whatever shows up accidentally, will be without a plan. This is not your case. You were promised. Everything concerning your life was already sorted out. Jesus was promised. When He showed up, He said: *"I only came to fulfill what was written of Me"* **(Luke 24:44).**

God does not do things erratically. If you understand this, you will realize then that there is no reason to fret. There is no reason to be bothered. There is no reason to go into anxiety or depression or anything like that because you know you are a child of promise.

Revisiting our main text in this chapter, Genesis 17:9 *"And God said to Abraham, as for you, you shall keep my covenant, you, and your descendants after you throughout their generations..."* Is it only Abraham who is supposed to keep the covenant? No. It says you and your descendants after you, throughout their whole generation.

THERE ARE CONDITIONS

So, in every generation, the covenant has to be kept. I know some people have said that the Abrahamic covenant is an unconditional covenant. I do not fully agree with that. There is a dimension of truth in it, but it is not the fullness of truth. There is still a condition; you need to give yourself totally to the Lord before you can say you are in a covenant. You cannot say you are in a covenant, and you are walking in ways that are against the one with whom you are covenanted. The covenant demands that you keep your end of the bargain and the other keeps the end of his bargain.

The circumcision that the Lord spoke to Abraham about was a sign of the covenant. Now, look at a typical example; In the natural world, people who make blood covenants with themselves, cut themselves and mix their blood. This is what they did in the primitive days. In those days, the parties cut themselves and mixed their blood and become covenanted. Then they declare and speak over one another, and if it is with a god, they do it in its presence.

Now, the covenant in itself is what they have declared to one another. But the scar that is left becomes their sign of the covenant. Now the scar in itself is not the condition of the covenant, it is only the sign that they entered the covenant. So, whenever they look at this scar, they remember that they entered into a covenant with somebody.

So, it is the same principle that we need to bear in mind concerning circumcision. The circumcision, as it were, was a sign, but the real deal or the condition of the keeping of the covenant was a heart that was totally given to God in Genesis 15. Abraham gave God what we call a total surrender, a total abandonment. He totally gave him everything of himself in that context, which I have tried to establish in previous chapters.

OBEDIENCE

Obedience is the greatest virtue. Now we will look at other Scriptures to buttress this because the Lord spoke to me personally about this. He said the greatest attribute He is looking for in His children is Obedience.

I realized that one of the hallmarks of Abraham is obedience. He walked in total and complete obedience even when the circumstances were not favorable. When God told him to sacrifice Isaac, he obeyed.

What God is asking for from His children and from those who will walk in the Abrahamic covenant with Him is obedience as a lifestyle; your ability to say, 'I give myself totally to You, God, and I will obey every word of Your instruction'.

If it is written in the Book, I am going to obey it. If You say I should, I will. If You say I should do this, I will do it. If You say go there, I will go there.

You cannot say that you are a believer, yet you are not digging into the Word of God. The Word of God in the Bible is the term of your contract. They are the terms of your agreement, and the more you understand this, the more you know what to claim, or what to do or not do. No wonder when the devil came to Jesus, Jesus understood the terms of the covenant, and He declared according to what is written.

Now when we go to Romans chapter four verse three, still talking about keeping God's covenant or the Abrahamic covenant, the Scripture says, "*Abraham believed God, and it was accounted to him for righteousness.*"

Where did we first find that Scripture? Genesis 15 verse 6. So, we can see there that Abraham believed God and it was accounted to him for righteousness. That was the reference point. The reference point was not necessarily circumcision per se. It was the fact that he believed in God from the place of total surrender. Then he said:

"*Now to him who works, the wages are not counted as grace but as debt. But to him who does not work but believes on Him who justifies the ungodly, his faith is accounted for righteousness.*" **(vv4-5)**

This is the mindset that Abraham had which Paul is revealing here. If it was not in the context of what God was saying, when we read it, we will think that all God was saying was how he is going to have so many children. But what Abraham was looking at was a lot more than that. It was giving his total self to the Lord. It was releasing himself to God saying, "God, You are my covenant partner, You are everything, You are the one that justifies the ungodly"

"...for we say that faith was accounted to Abraham as for righteousness."

Because circumcision in itself is of no use. It is just a seal. It is total obedience and total surrender to God that is the keeping of the covenant. Verse 27-29 says:

"And will not the physically uncircumcised, if he fulfills the law, judge you who, even with your written code and circumcision, are a transgressor of the law? For he is not a Jew who is one outwardly, nor is circumcision that which is outward in the flesh: but he is a Jew who is one inwardly; and circumcision is that of the heart, in the Spirit, not in the letter."

So, when Abraham was keeping the covenant of God, he was keeping the covenant based on the simple fact that he gave himself totally to the Lord. Today, if we claim we are going to walk in the blessings of Abraham, we must surrender ourselves to God completely.

THE CONDITION

The condition is obedience; ***if you obey My voice, and keep My covenant...*** The keeping of the covenant is tied to the issue of obedience. Child of God, if there is something that you need to engrave on your neck and in your heart, it is obedience. This year and hereafter, always walk in obedience to the Lord, even when it is inconvenient; even when it is not the most popular thing that is going on, I will walk in obedience to the Lord.

I believe that the Lord is calling His house to obedience. I believe that the Lord is calling His body to obedience. I believe the Lord is calling His people back to that place of total trust and total surrender. The Lord is calling His children and saying, Will you trust Me? Will you believe Me? Will you follow what I say? Will you follow My lead? That is what He is crying out and saying that His children should do today.

So, you now realize what Romans 4:12 goes on to say towards the latter part starting from verse 12, he said, "*And the father of circumcision, to those who not only are of the circumcision,* (that is Abraham) *but who also walk in the steps of faith, which our father Abraham had, while he still was uncircumcised.*"

The obedience that Abraham demonstrated is what He is asking everyone to do and demonstrate if we are to walk with the Lord. I hope the point is clear. If the point is clear enough, then we can now understand Deuteronomy 28 a lot better. These are the words of the Lord tied to the Abrahamic covenant. He says in there:

Now it will be if you diligently obey the voice of the LORD your God. Being careful to do all his commandments which I command you today, then the Lord your God will set you high above the nations of the earth, and all these blessings will come upon you and overtake you because you obey the voice of the Lord your God." **(Deuteronomy 28:1&2).**

Obedience unlocks your covenant. Obedience unlocks the covenant blessing. It unlocks the covenant promise. Obedience is key. Even the seed of Abraham, Jesus Christ Himself when he came, got to that point where he said "I did not come to do My will; I came to do the will of the One that sent Me..., by Myself I do not judge but only what I hear that I judge..., I must work the work of Him that sent Me while it is day because the night will come and no man can work".

He is doing the work of Him that sent Him. He walked in obedience. Even when He got to the place where it was difficult to go through, in the Garden of Gethsemane, He said, "if only this cup will pass me by, but not My will but Your will be done". He went through obedience even though it was difficult. Beloved, wants you to enjoy the covenant Blessings, are you ready to surrender to Him? The Blessings of God are for those who keep His commandments.

The blessing of the covenant covers all aspects of life, and I will paste down the blessing of Deuteronomy 28 from the Message Translation:

"If you listen obediently to the Voice of God, your God, and heartily obey all his commandments that I command you today, God, your God, will place you on high, high above all the nations of the world. All these blessings will come down on you and spread out beyond you because you have responded to the Voice of God, your God:

God's blessing inside the city, God's blessing in the country; God's blessing on your children, the crops of your land, the young of your livestock, the calves of your herds, the lambs of your flocks. God's blessing on your basket and bread bowl; God's blessing in your coming in, God's blessing in your going out.

God will defeat your enemies who attack you. They'll come at you on one road and run away on seven roads.

God will order a blessing on your barns and workplaces; he'll bless you in the land that God, your God, is giving you.

God will form you as a people holy to him, just as he promised you, if you keep the commandments of God, your God, and live the way he has shown you.

All the peoples on Earth will see you living under the Name of God and hold you in respectful awe.

*God will lavish you with good things: children from your womb, offspring from your animals, and crops from your land, the land that God promised your ancestors that he would give you. God will throw open the doors of his sky vaults and pour rain on your land on schedule and bless the work you take in hand. You will lend to many nations but you yourself won't have to take out a loan. God will make you the head, not the tail; you'll always be the top dog, never the underdog, as you obediently listen to and diligently keep the commands of God, your God, that I am commanding you today. Don't swerve an inch to the right or left from the words that I command you today by going off following and worshiping other gods." (**vv1-14**)*

CHAPTER TEN

COVENANT KEEPING GOD

"He is the Lord our God; His judgments are in all the earth. He remembers His covenant forever, the word which He commanded, for a thousand generations, the covenant which He made with Abraham, and His oath to Isaac, and confirmed it to Jacob for a statute, to Israel as an everlasting covenant, saying, "To you I will give the land of Canaan as the allotment of your inheritance" (**Psalm 105:7-11**)

"For He remembered His holy promise, and Abraham His servant. He brought out His people with joy, His chosen ones with gladness. He gave them the lands of the Gentiles, and they inherited the labour of the nations, that they might observe His statutes and keep His laws. Praise the Lord!" (**Psalm 105:42-25**)

We often sing songs about God being a covenant-keeping God. However, many people may not know the Scripture that backs up this truth, and even more importantly, many do not live their lives knowing that if God has said something or made a covenant on something, He sticks to it.

From Psalm 105 in our text, we can conclude the following:

1. ***God remembers His covenant forever...*** He made a covenant with Abraham, and He remembers it; He made the New Covenant through Jesus Christ, and He remembers it! He will not make a covenant and then forget about it. He is the

God who makes a covenant and remembers it forever. The blessings and promises attached to the covenant are not forgotten by God.

2. ***To a thousand generations, the word of God stands...*** In the sight of God, His promise and covenant are the same! If God makes a promise, it is as good as He cutting a covenant on that matter.

To a thousand generations, the word of God stands. The covenant of God, the promise, and the word of God stands. God's covenant and God's promise are not different from each other. When God promises you something, he will fulfill his promise. When God makes a covenant with you, he fulfills the covenant terms. So, when the Bible says, 'to a thousand generations', the word of God stands, it means that God remembers his word even for a thousand generations and beyond. He made a covenant with Abraham and generations after him, and he is still fulfilling that promise in the lives of his children, even in our own lives today.

3. ***The purpose of God's Covenants (no matter the covenant) is to bring His people closer to Him or develop an intimacy with Him.*** All of God's covenants with people are to create dependency on Him and not independence.

The purpose of God's covenant is to bring us closer to him. God has not given us a covenant that will make us independent of him, but a covenant that will make us dependent on him. If at the end of the day, you are claiming God's covenant promises, but he has nothing to do with your personal relationship with him or coming closer to him, it is almost an illegal way to maximize the covenant. The covenant must involve you coming closer and deeper with God. If you look at Genesis 17:7, where he made a covenant with Abraham, he said that he would establish his covenant between himself, Abraham, and Abraham's descendants for an everlasting covenant, to be their God.

Though there are other blessings, such as the land and things that we inherit, the covenant includes that he must be God over them. Sometimes, what hinders the manifestation in our lives is the motives behind some of the desires that we have. When our motives are distant from the connection that God is looking for, the promise we are asking for is almost as if we are asking for it illegally. The best illustration for this is when someone desires intimacy and then goes to get it illegally when they could get it within the context of marriage. When God says that he will be their God, then the promise that he has given them in their covenant is only legal within the context that he remains their God. The children of Israel struggled with this, as when they departed from God, the Abrahamic promises and blessings were not manifesting in their lives. They became captives, served other people, and went through difficult times because they went outside of the terms of the covenant.

In Jeremiah 31:33, it is stated that God will put His law in the minds of the people of Israel and write it on their hearts, and that He will be their God and they will be His people. It is important to understand that this covenant requires intimacy, and that God never breaks His promises. He will fulfill His promises to us.

This same truth is affirmed in Psalm 89:

"My covenant I will not break, nor alter the word that has gone out of My lips. Once I have sworn by My holiness; I will not lie to David: His seed shall endure forever, and his throne as the sun before Me; It shall be established forever like the moon, even like the faithful witness in the sky." Selah" (**Psalm 89:34-37**)

1. ***God will never break His covenant.*** He has made a covenant with you through Jesus Christ, and that covenant stands forever... His covenant, He will not break.

This means that when God has made a promise to us in any area of life, He will fulfill it and will not go back on His word. We must stand firm on the promises of God because they are the now word of God for us, even if the circumstances around us seem to contradict them. We must choose to believe the Word of God and not be swayed by the opinions or reports of others. We must also be consistent in our beliefs and not waver in our faith. It is important to stay focused on the promises of God and not allow ourselves to become double-minded.

2. ***God will not alter His words...*** Confirming what we have read before, God used the most permanent stuff that humans can relate to as a confirmation that His word will stand. He used the Sun, the Moon, and the Sky. Except those fail, then His words will fail.

3. ***God swore to assure the recipients of His covenant...*** God said: "Once I have sworn in My holiness..." This swearing is not to validate God's word or Person, but to assure the recipients of the covenant promises and blessings.

Because life happens to David as it happens to your life, life happens to Abraham as it happens to you. The Bible said concerning Abraham, in Genesis 22:16, "By Myself I have sworn." God could not find anyone greater than himself. So, He now said to Abraham in my paraphrase, 'by myself, I swear to you that what I said I will do, I will do.' God was not swearing because of his own nature; it is impossible, he is perfect. But He was swearing so that Abraham might know without a shadow of doubt that what He has said He would do, He will do. And to David, he said in my paraphrase, 'once have I sworn in my holiness, that so far, I am

God, this word will stand. If this word fails, then I am no longer God.' Now, that is something. That seed is Jesus Christ. And He is still on the throne today. To reassure us, God said, I will swear. I will swear and He swore to Abraham and He swore to David. These two covenants (Abrahamic and Davidic) are the bedrock of the new covenant.

God will never break His word, His covenant, and the promises associated with them. We can see the prophecy of Isaiah alluding to the same truth:

"For My thoughts are not your thoughts, nor are your ways My ways," says the Lord. "For as the heavens are higher than the earth, so are My ways higher than your ways, and My thoughts than your thoughts. "For as the rain comes down, and the snow from heaven, and do not return there, but water the earth, and make it bring forth and bud, that it may give seed to the Sower and bread to the eater, so shall My word be that goes forth from My mouth; It shall not return to Me void, but it shall accomplish what I please, and it shall prosper in the thing for which I sent it." (***Isaiah 55:8-11***)

The word that comes from God's mouth will not return to Him empty or without effect. It will accomplish what He desires and will succeed in the purpose for which it was sent. This is a powerful promise and reminder of the authority and reliability of God's word. It is something we can stand on and trust in as we seek the fulfillment of the covenant promises and plans that God has for our lives.

Again, I will highlight three points from these verses in Isaiah 55.

1. ***Your thoughts are lower (far lower) than God's thoughts.*** Your thoughts can change, vary, be unsettled etc. but God's thoughts are pure, holy, and fixed for your benefit.

Your thoughts may be trying to figure out how something will happen or seeking help from others. But God's thoughts are unlimited, without any concept of limitation. Hence, we should have the mind of Christ that is able to comprehend the fullness of God's thoughts as our thoughts.

2. ***Your ways are much lower than God's ways.*** No matter how you try to figure it out by yourself; have all the education and intelligence known to man, it is inferior to the ways of God. His ways are steady, powerful, fruitful, and fulfilling.

Our ways can be unstable, crooked, or prone to compromise, but God's ways are perfect, pure, sure, and straight. God is the same yesterday, today, and forever, and His ways do not change.

3. ***God said, "the words that comes out from my mouth will not return to me unfulfilled"***. God watches over His word to fulfill it.

The words that come out of God's mouth will not return to Him unfulfilled. If God speaks a word over your life, it will come to pass. Don't let fear or doubt hold you back from receiving and believing in God's promises for you. Remember, you have been called to believe, not just to understand. Trust in God's good plans for you and His Word will come to pass.

So, when God speaks a word of promise over your life, don't let fear or doubt hold you back from receiving it. Trust in God's good plans for you and His Word will come to pass. Sometimes, we may not understand everything, but we have been called to believe in what God has revealed to us. And when we stand on His promises and His Word, no matter what the world may throw at us, we know that God has good thoughts toward us, and His Word will come to pass.

When my son was born, the doctors gave us a terrible report with loads of abnormalities with the pregnancy and suggested we abort the pregnancy. But we looked at each other and said no because we knew that God's Word says we are fearfully and wonderfully made. When the child was born, he was perfect, and the doctors couldn't find any of the problems they had predicted. This is because there is a God in heaven who rules over the affairs of men. It doesn't matter what man may say, God's Word is final. When you stand on His promise and His Word, nothing can shake you. God will keep His covenant promises.

We can look at more scriptures affirming the same point. God will keep His covenant and the promises attached to them. In Jeremiah 1:12, God said I am actively watching over My word to perform or fulfill it.

*"The word of the Lord came to me, saying, "Jeremiah, what do you see?" And I said, "I see the branch of an almond tree." Then the Lord said to me, "You have seen well, for I am [actively] watching over My word to fulfil it." (**Jeremiah 1:11-12 AMP**)*

These are scriptures upon scriptures confirming the same. God will not forget His covenant, and neither will He break them. His words and promises stand forever, and He watches over them to fulfill them. In Christ, all the promises of God already have an answer of "YES", so our response is "Amen" to all of God's covenant promises.

*"For as many as are the promises of God, in Christ they are [all answered] "Yes." So, through Him we say our "Amen" to the glory of God." (**2 Corinthians 1:20 AMP**)*

This was the testimony of the Children of Israel after they had taken possession of the land God promised them through the Abrahamic Covenant and fulfilled in the time of Moses and Joshua:

"So, the Lord gave to Israel all the land of which He had sworn to give to their fathers, and they took possession of it and dwelt in it. The Lord gave them rest all around, according to all that He had sworn to their fathers. And not a man of all their enemies stood against them; the Lord delivered all their enemies into their hand. Not a word failed of any good thing which the Lord had spoken to the house of Israel. All came to pass." (**Joshua 21:43-45**)

Therefore, if the above is true and you believe that God will fulfill His promise and never break His covenant, then faith should become easier for you and me.

In concluding this chapter, we visit Galatians 3 where it is clearly stated that the blessing of Abraham will come upon the gentile, believers in Christ, as long as they belong to Christ.

"Christ has redeemed us from the curse of the law, having become a curse for us (for it is written, "Cursed is everyone who hangs on a tree"), that the blessing of Abraham might come upon the Gentiles in Christ Jesus, that we might receive the promise of the Spirit through faith." (**Galatians 3:13-14**)

The Blessing of Abraham has come upon me – the gentile (believer in Jesus) who is now the New Israel.

What then is the blessing of Abraham? What is that to you and to me? This becomes the assignment of every believer in Christ to study and know the contents of this "blessing" so that they might be able to appropriate or believe them.

Here, some examples include:

"And you shall remember the Lord your God, for it is He who gives you power to get wealth, that He may establish His covenant which He swore to your fathers, as it is this day." (**Deuteronomy 8:18**)

- God gives you the power to get wealth that He might establish His covenant. God wants to manifest His covenant and He requires you and me to "remember". This is a call to intimacy with the Lord (a lifestyle of obedience) – and when this is done, He will give you the power to get wealth.

"Grace and peace be multiplied to you in the knowledge of God and of Jesus our Lord, as His divine power has given to us all things that pertain to life and godliness, through the knowledge of Him who called us by glory and virtue, by which have been given to us exceedingly great and precious promises, that through these you may be partakers of the divine nature, having escaped the corruption that is in the world through lust." (**2 Peter 1:2-4**)

- By the divine power of our Lord Jesus, we have been given all things that pertain to life and godliness. What are the things you require that pertain to living life? It has been given! What are the things that pertain to godliness in your life, it has been given.
- He has given to us exceedingly great and precious promises...and through these promises, we become partakers of the divine nature. By covenant, our nature is divine!!!

"With long life I will satisfy him and show him My salvation." (**Psalm 91:16**)

- Long life is a covenant promise... Do we believe it?

"So, you shall serve the Lord your God, and He will bless your bread and your water. And I will take sickness away from the midst of you. No one shall suffer miscarriage or be barren in your land; I will fulfil the number of your days." (**Exodus 23:25-26**)

- The promise stands – God will bless your bread and water. It is a colloquial term like we use today saying "It is my bread and butter". Everything that is for your day-to-day living is blessed by the Lord.

- God will take sickness away from the midst of you. Again, a covenant promise.
- No one among us will suffer miscarriage neither will anyone be barren in our land. It is a covenant promise.
- The number of our days, God will help us fulfil.

These are promises and more... God is a covenant-keeping God. He keeps and fulfills His covenant. Pray! Believe! Trust

CHAPTER ELEVEN

GOD'S COVENANT OF LIFE

Bless the Lord, O my soul; And all that is within me, bless His holy name! Bless the Lord, O my soul, and forget not all His benefits: Who forgives all your iniquities, who heals all your diseases, who redeems your life from destruction, Who crowns you with loving-kindness and tender mercies, Who satisfies your mouth with good things, So that your youth is renewed like the eagle's ***(Psalm 103:1-5).***

The central focus of the covenants of God with man is always about the life of man. The essence of the covenant is an assurance from God that he has your life in his hands. If you have been experiencing fear or worry about your life, know that God has got you and nothing can take your life before its time or stop you from living the fullness of life that God has planned for you. The center focus of God's covenants is on the life of the individual where He is saying, this is the life that I want you to live.

The thief does not come except to steal, and to kill, and to destroy. I have come that they may have life, and that they may have it more abundantly ***(John 10:10).***

Why did Jesus come? Can you personalize it? He came because of me; to give me life and not just any type of life but abundant life.

THE MEDIATOR OF THE BETTER COVENANT

Jesus is the mediator of the better covenant based on better promises (Hebrews 8:6). He made it very clear to all that He came so all may have life. There are many that are living in fear of death or subservient life, but that is not the plan of God for you. God did not plan that you live a life of fear and intimidation. God's plan for you is that you live a life that is abundant and full.

"Therefore, since [these His] children share in flesh and blood [the physical nature of mankind], He Himself in a similar manner also shared in the same [physical nature, but without sin], so that through [experiencing] death He might make powerless (ineffective, impotent) him who had the power of death—that is, the devil—and [that He] might free all those who through [the haunting] fear of death were held in slavery throughout their lives. For, as we all know, He (Christ) does not take hold of [the fallen] angels [to give them a helping hand], but He does take hold of [the fallen] descendants of Abraham [extending to them His hand of deliverance]." (**Hebrews 2:14-16 AMP**)

Reading from Hebrews 2 above, the essence of the new covenant comes up where Jesus manifested in the physical nature of fallen man but without sin of His own. This was to make powerless, ineffective, and impotent the power of the devil who had power over death, thereby delivering the descendants of Abraham from a lifetime of bondage and fear of death.

I can tell you that because of the new covenant, you have been delivered from the root of all fear which ultimately is the fear of death. Hence, the Bible will assure us that God has not given us the spirit of fear because fear is a spirit – a tormenting, haunting, and terrible spirit, but God has given us the Spirit of love, power, and of a sound mind.

"For God did not give us a spirit of timidity or cowardice or fear, but [He has given us a spirit] of power and of love and of sound judgment and personal discipline [abilities that result in a calm, well-balanced mind and self-control]." (**2 Timothy 1:7 AMP**)

The life that God has ordained for every of His child is a life that is abundant and full. Not of fear, timidity, inadequacy, or a life of limitation. There are many scriptures that talk about the abundant life.

"With long life I will satisfy him and show him My salvation" **(Psalm 91:16).**

This is God's covenant statement. Nothing can take your life. No disease or sickness can take your life; no accidents can take your life. I declare that over you now and for the rest of your life, nothing can take your life, nothing will take the life of your children, nothing will take the life of your spouse. They will live the fullness of life in the name of Jesus Christ.

"With long life, I will satisfy him".

The simple interpretation of this statement is when you are satisfied, you can then go to be with the Lord. You could age to a point where you decide to leave.

"I shall not die but live to declare the works of the Lord" **(Psalm 118: 17).**

The psalmist said this of Himself. You have got to declare Words in harmony with the covenant to live the full and abundant life. If the angels of God were going to take your words to God, what will they take for you?

You must speak life and not death no matter how you feel. I must live! Your body must live! Your organs must live! Your brain must live! It doesn't matter what part of your body, it got to live because God created it with life. His plan is that every part of you must Live.

In Exodus 23:25-26

"So, you shall serve the Lord your God, and He will bless your bread and your water. And I will take sickness away from the midst of you."

This is a covenant promise. God says He **WILL** take away sickness from the midst of you. This includes our family, household, and everywhere around us.

There is no sickness or disease, in the name of Jesus, everyone reading this right now, whether you are visiting the doctor or consultant, you are being discharged in the name of Jesus because God has said **"I will take sickness away from the midst of you."**

Verse 26 *"No one shall suffer miscarriage or be barren in your land; I will fulfill the number of your days."*

Who will fulfill the number of your days? God.

The Lord said He will fulfill it. If He said it then, He would do it. He is not a man that should lie or the son of man that will change His mind.

I pray that deliverance comes to you because of the covenant word of God as you believe and receive it.

Just because others have died prematurely should not make you loosen your hold on the faithfulness of God's promises. It could be the same diagnosis that somebody else had and they died but if it touches your body, it will die rather than you. The experience of others is not your yardstick. Your yardstick is the word of God who cannot lie nor repent. We may not be able to explain to other people, but what we know is that we stand on the authenticity of the Word of God.

We know that we serve a covenant-keeping God. He says in his Word, "*My covenant I will not break*". God will never break His covenant. So, you must hold tightly to the covenant promise of a full and abundant life. It doesn't matter whatsoever that is speaking contrary to your life right now, you must resist it with the covenant promise.

Everything speaking contrary to your wealth and prosperity, you must resist it. My mother may have died of this, but I will not die of it. My brothers and sisters may have died of this, but I will not in the name of Jesus. I stand on the covenant of the Word of God, that the same God that watches over His word to perform it will watch over His word to perform it over my life in the name of Jesus Christ.

Others may apply and not get it, but not you. Others may try and it didn't happen for them but not you. Others may be messed up but not you. Somebody may say there is a casting down, but I live in the camp of those that say there is a lifting up.

We are they that were purchased by the precious Blood of Jesus Christ. Therefore, I declare every voice speaking contrary to your life and purpose is silenced in the name of Jesus. We were bought with the precious blood of Jesus Christ. This is the new covenant of life. This happened so that you live an overcoming life and not a life of fear and intimidation. Your destiny is not in the hands of any human being but of God. *Who is he who speaks, and it comes to pass, when the Lord has not commanded it? (Lamentations 3:37)*

People will come with phone calls and be telling you things that are happening in the negative, but you must not confess the same with them. They will be speaking things that will make you speak in a negative way; you must not confess the same thing with them because your story is different. You are under the covenant of Christ; therefore your confession must be along the same line as the covenant promises of God.

Mark the Clear Difference:

- God will always speak of life and manifest life...and more life.
- The devil will speak death, sickness, disease etc...and more misery.

We cannot confuse the ministry of God and the ministry of the devil. God will always speak life, manifest life, and do all that is necessary for you to live an abundant life, however, the devil will manifest death, sickness, disease, demonization etc.

We can therefore categorically declare:

- Anything that speaks contrary to life, I will resist.
- Anything that speaks contrary to health, I will resist.
- Anything that speaks contrary to well-being, I will resist.
- Anything that speaks contrary to wealth and prosperity, I will resist.
- Anything that speaks contrary to an "overcoming lifestyle", I will firmly resist.

Now, when we are talking about the covenant of life, I want us to understand in a little dimension. The psalmist starts in Psalm 103:1-5 that we read with the words: *"Who forgives all your iniquities, who heals all your diseases"* ***(Psalms 103:3).***

That is the beginning, when we are talking about the covenant of life, the first thing is forgiveness. You don't have life until you're forgiven, you don't have life until your iniquities are purged. Biblically, anyone who sins is not forgiven, that is, anyone who has not received Jesus as his/her Lord and Savior is considered dead. They are spiritually dead and have a need of life. The life only Jesus can give. Therefore, when you receive Jesus as your Lord and Savior, you move from death to life. (John 5:24)

So, the first access to life is to bid goodbye to the devil's kingdom and have your sins purged by Christ's blood and receive forgiveness. None of us is entitled to forgiveness. Forgiveness is not a right but part of the grace of the abundant life that God has promised. He said, I'll forgive you. All you just need to do is to ask for it.

The second aspect of the abundant life is healing.

"Who forgives all your iniquities, who heals all your diseases" ***(Psalms 103:3).***

Healing from all sickness and diseases, is part of the abundant life that Jesus paid for and therefore, part of the new covenant. In fact, in the earthly ministry of Jesus, He spent most of His time healing the sick and delivering the oppressed. You don't have to have disease and sicknesses in your body or even in your mind because Jesus came so you might have life and have it in abundance. This is the covenant of life.

One of the stories in the Bible where Jesus insisted that He heals because the recipient is covenanted is in Luke 13. Let us read below:

"Now He was teaching in one of the synagogues on the Sabbath. And behold, there was a woman who had a spirit of infirmity eighteen years and was bent over and could in no way raise herself up. But when Jesus saw her, He called her to Him and said to her, "Woman, you are loosed from your infirmity." And He laid His hands on her, and immediately she was made straight, and glorified God. But the ruler of the synagogue answered with indignation, because Jesus had healed on the Sabbath; and he said to the crowd, "There are six days on which men ought to work; therefore, come and be healed on them, and not on the Sabbath day." The Lord then answered him and said, "Hypocrite! Does not each one of you on the Sabbath loose his ox or donkey from the stall, and lead it away to

water it? So, ought not this woman, being a daughter of Abraham, whom Satan has bound—think of it—for eighteen years, be loosed from this bond on the Sabbath?" And when He said these things, all His adversaries were put to shame; and all the multitude rejoiced for all the glorious things that were done by Him." (**Luke 13:10-17**)

Jesus wanted this woman to live the abundant life that He has for her. The devil has afflicted this woman for 18 years and could not enjoy her covenant blessing of divine health and perhaps, also hindered her from enjoying the fullness of life. Jesus healed this woman by casting out from her the spirit of infirmity. The beautiful part of this story for me is Jesus' reply to the ruler of the synagogue saying: *"So, ought not this woman, being a daughter of Abraham, whom Satan has bound—think of it—for eighteen years, be loosed from this bond on the Sabbath?"* She is indeed the daughter of Abraham hence she is covenanted and entitled to be healed from her infirmities.

The third aspect of the psalmist's declaration is that the Lord is the one *"who redeems your life from destruction"*. You have received redemption from destruction to life. There are those whose lives right now is not what God planned for them by covenant. Their lives are in a downward spiral of destruction. To live the life of God that God intends for you, you need to receive the redemption God is giving you right now by covenant.

There are those who are hooked on drugs, alcohol, sex, destructive behavior, and irresponsible lifestyles, etc., God is saying to you right now... receive His redemption. Choose to be free. God's covenant life is free from the lifestyle of destruction. See another record in the book of Luke.

"Now it came to pass, afterward, that He went through every city and village, preaching and bringing the glad tidings of the kingdom of God. And the twelve were with Him, and certain women who had

been healed of evil spirits and infirmities—Mary called Magdalene, out of whom had come seven demons, and Joanna the wife of Chuza, Herod's steward, and Susanna, and many others who provided for Him from their substance." (**Luke 8:1-3**)

These women were on the path of destruction until they met Jesus, and their lives changed.

The fourth aspect of this psalmist declaration I will call attention to is in verse 5 where it is recorded: *"Who satisfies your mouth with good things, so that your youth is renewed like the eagle's".* God wants us to receive of the Lord things until we are satisfied. This is God's plan and the meaning of covenant life of God. The Bible encourages you to receive of the Lord "good things" until you are satisfied.

Have you been satisfied yet with all the "good things" the Lord has for you?

What will be the use of life if the very good things that are promised in the covenant of God for us are not in manifestation? God has given to us based on the new covenant, all things that pertain to life and godliness, therefore, it is imperative that we lay hold of them.

Two scriptures that mean so much to me are these:

"The young lions lack and suffer hunger; But those who seek the Lord shall not lack any good thing." (**Psalm 34:10**)

"For the Lord God is a sun and shield; The Lord will give grace and glory; No good thing will He withhold from those who walk uprightly." (**Psalm 84:11**)

God's good is waiting for you and me. It is part of His covenant for your life.

I want to reiterate this point one more time before I conclude this chapter. Be careful of your confession, what you say empowers the angels of God or empowers demons. What you say empowers the angels of God or disarms them. When you pray but you speak out contrary to what you have prayed, then you become a double-minded man, so you shouldn't expect to receive anything from God. The covenant of Life that you have is that you live a healthy, wealthy, and contented life in Christ Jesus.

CHAPTER TWELVE

ASSURANCE OF THE COVENANT

"As for you, if you walk before Me as your father David walked, and do according to all that I have commanded you, and if you keep My statutes and My judgments, then I will establish the throne of your kingdom, as I covenanted with David your father, saying, 'You shall not fail to have a man as ruler in Israel.'" (**2 Chronicles 7:17-18**)

Following from the previous chapter, we see God in the verses above assuring Solomon that the covenanted words spoken by Him to David will be fulfilled as long as Solomon does not seek other gods. Well, Solomon sought other gods and abandoned Jehovah, God of Israel, and yet because of God's covenant with David, God will not wipe off the lineage of David from ruling despite Solomon's actions. God still kept one tribe in the lineage of David because of the covenant.

"For it was so, when Solomon was old, that his wives turned his heart after other gods; and his heart was not loyal to the Lord his God, as was the heart of his father David. For Solomon went after Ashtoreth the goddess of the Sidonians, and after Milcom the abomination of the Ammonites. Solomon did evil in the sight of the Lord, and did not fully follow the Lord, as did his father David.... So the Lord became angry with Solomon, because his heart had turned from the Lord God of Israel, who had appeared to him twice, and had commanded him concerning this thing, that he should not go after other gods; but he did not keep what the Lord had

commanded. Therefore, the Lord said to Solomon, "Because you have done this, and have not kept My covenant and My statutes, which I have commanded you, I will surely tear the kingdom away from you and give it to your servant. Nevertheless, I will not do it in your days, for the sake of your father David; I will tear it out of the hand of your son. However, I will not tear away the whole kingdom; I will give one tribe to your son for the sake of My servant David, and for the sake of Jerusalem which I have chosen." (1 Kings 11:4-6; 9-13).

From my study of the Bible, the best way to explain God's assurances regarding His covenant and covenant promises is to review the Hebrews records of the Abrahamic covenant.

For the purposes of clarity, I will include the Passion Translation of the Hebrews passage together with my default NKJV version.

"And we desire that each one of you show the same diligence to the full assurance of hope until the end, that you do not become sluggish, but imitate those who through faith and patience inherit the promises. For when God made a promise to Abraham because He could swear by no one greater, He swore by Himself, saying, "Surely blessing I will bless you, and multiplying I will multiply you." And so, after he had patiently endured, he obtained the promise. For men indeed swear by the greater, and an oath for confirmation is for them an end of all dispute. Thus God, determining to show more abundantly **to the heirs of promise** *the immutability of His counsel, confirmed it by an oath, that by two immutable things, in which it is impossible for God to lie, we might have strong consolation, who have fled for refuge to lay hold of the hope set before us."* (**Hebrews 6:11-18**)

"But we long to see you passionately advance until the end and you find your hope fulfilled. So don't allow your hearts to grow dull or lose your enthusiasm but follow the example of those who fully received what God has promised because of their strong faith and

patient endurance. Now when God made a promise to Abraham, since there was no one greater than himself, he swore an oath on his own integrity to keep the promise as sure as God exists! So, he said, "Have no doubt, I promise to bless you over and over, and give you a son and multiply you without measure!" So, Abraham waited patiently in faith and succeeded in seeing the promise fulfilled. It is very common for people to swear an oath by something greater than themselves, for the oath will confirm their statements and end all dispute. So, in the same way, God wanted to end all doubt and confirm it even more forcefully to those who would inherit his promises. His purpose was unchangeable, so God added his vow to the promise. So, it is impossible for God to lie for we know that his promise and his vow will never change! And now we have run into his heart to hide ourselves in his faithfulness. This is where we find his strength and comfort, for he empowers us to seize what has already been established ahead of time—an unshakable hope!" ***(vv11-18 TPT)***

God wanted to give an assurance (even more abundantly) to the heirs of the promise, He decided that He will confirm it by an oath – thereby by two immutable things (God's Promise and God's oath or vow), the covenant promises of God are rock solid guaranteed to the heirs of the promise.

These words were written to believers who were losing their faith, getting discouraged, and perhaps, having lost sight of the covenant they had with God. They needed to be assured and brought back to the word of God and the terms of the covenant and with that knowledge, they could run to God and hide in His faithfulness. God will fulfill what He has promised.

To make this chapter easy to study and assimilate, I have chosen to relay the contents of this chapter in a bullet point manner and hopefully, by this, we build a clear picture of God's intent in assuring us.

1. ***You are the heirs of the promise of the Abrahamic Covenant***

*"For you are all sons of God through faith in Christ Jesus. For as many of you as were baptized into Christ have put on Christ. There is neither Jew nor Greek, there is neither slave nor free, there is neither male nor female; for you are all one in Christ Jesus. And if you are Christ's, then you are Abraham's seed, and heirs according to the promise." (**Galatians 3:26-28**)*

Paul's letter to the Galatians confirms that since you are in Christ, then you are Abraham's seed and therefore, heirs according to the covenant promise. We have established this point in previous chapters.

2. ***God wants to leave you with no doubt that His covenant through Abraham for you is intact and cannot be annulled.***

In the verses we read, it is written: "*So, in the same way, God wanted to end all doubt and confirm it even more forcefully **to those who would inherit his promises**. His purpose was unchangeable, so God added his vow to the promise.*"

To confirm it to you and me, God said, "I will add a vow to my promise." God's promise is good enough and never fails, but for the sake of you and I, He added His vow to His promise...and thereby, by two immutable things, it is impossible for God to get out of this. He must fulfill His covenant promises, so long as we have fulfilled our terms of the covenant.

3. ***God wants your hope and faith to rest in His faithfulness to His promises.***

The passion translation says: "*And now we have run into his heart to hide ourselves in his faithfulness. This is where we find his strength and comfort, for he empowers us to seize what has already been established ahead of time—an unshakable hope!"*

No matter what is happening in your life today, learn to run into God's heart and hide in His faithfulness...for it is there you will find strength and comfort for your journey ahead.

What is this Covenant Promise?

For when God made a promise to Abraham because He could swear by no one greater, He swore by Himself, saying, "Surely blessing I will bless you, and multiplying I will multiply you." And so, after he had patiently endured, he obtained the promise.

It is the BLESSING!

Paul puts it this way in the book of Galatians:

"Christ has redeemed us from the curse of the law, having become a curse for us (for it is written, "Cursed is everyone who hangs on a tree"), ***that the blessing of Abraham*** *might come upon the Gentiles in Christ Jesus, that we might receive the promise of the Spirit through faith." (**Galatians 3:13-14**)*

There is something that has happened in the body of Christ for a long time. It appears when talking about covenant promises and covenant blessings, it is somehow opposite to holiness and righteousness and all those aspects of intimacy with Christ. But they are one and the same thing. The same gospel that brings righteousness, brings blessings; the same gospel that brings holiness, brings prosperity; the same gospel and verse that speaks about "wounded for our transgression" is the same gospel and verse that speaks that "by His stripes, we are healed"; and the same gospel that talks about intimacy, brings people into the abundance of God. We have compartmentalized this in the church over the years, thinking that if you have one, you can't have the other. But that's not how the gospel was put together. It's meant to be all-encompassing and bring everything together. You can't be one without the other.

It's important to remember that the covenant promises of God are not just about material blessings or prosperity. While it is true that God blesses his people, the ultimate blessing is salvation through Jesus Christ and the promise of eternal life. The covenant promises of God also include the promise of forgiveness, the presence of the Holy Spirit, and the promise of being reconciled to God. It is through faith in Jesus and the power of the Holy Spirit that we can live holy and righteous lives, and it is through this faith that we can have confidence in the promises of God and receive the fullness of his blessings.

The blessing did not start with Abraham. The blessing started in the Garden of Eden; the moment God made man. The Bible said that God breathed into the nostrils of man and man became a living soul. So, the moment the man opened his eyes, what did man see? God, and when he saw God, the first word that came out of God is that you are blessed. So blessing was part of the design of God for man. You see, the blessing was in the design of God for man. So, when man fell (that is, fell into sin), man did not necessarily fall from the blessing. What man fell from is the glory. For all have sinned and fallen short of the glory of God (Romans 3:23). Man didn't fall from the blessing; he fell from the glory. When Jesus came, He restored man back to glory. But the blessing stood. So, when He spoke to Noah, he said, Noah, I will bless you just like I told Adam. When he spoke to Abraham, he said, I will bless you, like I told Adam. When He kept making covenants, He kept talking about the blessing, because through the blessing, is how a man is meant to function.

God was telling Abraham that he would not only be blessed but also be a blessing to others. Through Abraham, others would be blessed and would know what blessing looks like. It is not about chasing material possessions, but rather trusting in God for His blessings and allowing them to flow through us to bless others.

What is the Blessing?

There is no way we can answer the question without looking at the life of Abraham to see how he manifested the blessing. There is still so much to unpack with regard to Abraham and the blessing however, I have written here tasters and it is for you to study and let the Holy Spirit bring you into revelation as it applies to your life.

I will not go into full explanation or exploration of the various ways in which the blessing of the Lord manifests as it is beyond the scope of this book but rather highlight them as you explore these.

- ***The Blessing Manifests in Personal Relationship with God.***

*"Listen to Me, you who follow after righteousness, you who seek the Lord: Look to the rock from which you were hewn, and to the hole of the pit from which you were dug. Look to Abraham your father, and to Sarah who bore you; For I called him alone and blessed him and increased him." (**Isaiah 51:1-2**)*

*"And the Scripture was fulfilled which says, "Abraham believed God, and it was accounted to him for righteousness." And he was called the friend of God." (**James 2:23**)*

Blessedness is having that deep personal relationship with God. It is a state where you have access to God and your relationship with Him is thriving.

We see in the covenant discourse with Abraham in Genesis 17, God said: "I will be your God and God of your descendants after you…" – the blessing is a personal deep relationship with God.

If we view this in terms of access to God like the psalmist said: *"He who dwells in the secret place of the Most High shall abide under the shadow of the Almighty." (Psalm 91:1)*, it is a blessing and a massive privilege to dwell in the secret place of the Most High.

- **The Blessing Manifests in Finding Purpose in God**

*"When Abram was ninety-nine years old, the Lord appeared to Abram and said to him, "I am Almighty God; walk before Me and be blameless. And I will make My covenant between Me and you and will multiply you exceedingly." Then Abram fell on his face, and God talked with him, saying: "As for Me, behold, My covenant is with you, and you shall be a father of many nations." (**Genesis 17:1-4**)*

Abraham's purpose was to be a father of many nations. In the blessing, you find your purpose in God or your part in God's overall purpose. Life without a God-ordained purpose could be a wasted life. It is a blessing to know what you are called to do in God's overall plan in the world today.

- **The Blessing Manifests in Financial Prosperity**

*"Then Abram went up from Egypt, he, and his wife and all that he had, and Lot with him, to the South. Abram was very rich in livestock, in silver, and in gold." (**Genesis 13:1-2**)*

The Bible records that Abram was very rich in livestock, silver, and in gold. This same blessing can be ours as well. In previous chapters, we revealed God's intention in establishing His covenant by giving us power to make wealth as recorded in Deuteronomy 8:18.

- **The Blessing Manifests in Acquisition of Real Estate (Property, and Land)**

"And the Lord said to Abram, after Lot had separated from him: "Lift your eyes now and look from the place where you are—northward, southward, eastward, and westward; for all the land which you see I give to you and your descendants forever. And I will make your descendants as the dust of the earth; so that if a man could number the dust of the earth, then your descendants also could be numbered. Arise, walk in the land through its length and its width, for I give it to you."" (**Genesis 13:14-17**)

God gave Abram land. It was not just to Abram but also to his descendants that God gave land. Abraham nor his descendants had to pay for the land, properties, vineyards, etc. God gave it to them.

"So it shall be, when the Lord your God brings you into the land of which He swore to your fathers, to Abraham, Isaac, and Jacob, to give you large and beautiful cities which you did not build, houses full of all good things, which you did not fill, hewn-out wells which you did not dig, vineyards and olive trees which you did not plant—when you have eaten and are full... " (**Deuteronomy 6:10-11**)

It has nothing to do with what you can pay for but what the Lord gives you as a blessing due to His covenant.

- **The Blessing Manifests in Winning Battles**

"Then one who had escaped came and told Abram the Hebrew, for he dwelt by the terebinth trees of Mamre the Amorite, brother of Eshcol and brother of Aner; and they were allies with Abram. Now when Abram heard that his brother was taken captive, he armed his three hundred and eighteen trained servants who were born in his own house and went in pursuit as far as Dan. He divided his forces against them by night, and he and his servants attacked them and pursued them as far as Hobah, which is north of Damascus. So, he

brought back all the goods, and also brought back his brother Lot and his goods, as well as the women and the people." (**Genesis 14:13-16**)

Kings were fighting each other, and nations were fighting each other, however, since Lot was taken captive, it became Abraham's fight. The blessing manifested in Abraham winning the battle, bringing back all the goods, and brought back Lot and his goods... and the women and the people.

As I study the Bible, I see God rising up on behalf of His covenanted people and making them win battles that are naturally impossible for them to win. This is the manifestation of the blessing. Irrespective of the battles you face in life, know that you are covenanted and by virtue of this, you can call on the blessing to work for you.

- **The Blessing Manifests the Covenant Name**

"Then Melchizedek king of Salem brought out bread and wine; he was the priest of God Most High. And he blessed him and said: "Blessed be Abram of God Most High, Possessor of heaven and earth; And blessed be God Most High, Who has delivered your enemies into your hand." And he gave him a tithe of all." (**Genesis 14:18-20**)

Prior to the covenant with Abraham, there was nothing like "God of Abraham" which means God has taken the name of Abraham to be part of His. In this name, God is forever identified with the name Abraham. Genesis 14 above sees Abram being called "Abram of God Most High" which also means that Abram is now also described with the name of God Most High.

While this might not bear a direct relevance today, it however signifies how we can approach God based on the covenant name of God – God of Abraham.

- **The Blessing Manifests as Righteousness of God**

"After these things the word of the Lord came to Abram in a vision, saying, "Do not be afraid, Abram. I am your shield, your exceedingly great reward." But Abram said, "Lord God, what will You give me, seeing I go childless, and the heir of my house is Eliezer of Damascus?" Then Abram said, "Look, You have given me no offspring; indeed one born in my house is my heir!" And behold, the word of the Lord came to him, saying, "This one shall not be your heir, but one who will come from your own body shall be your heir." Then He brought him outside and said, "Look now toward heaven, and count the stars if you are able to number them." And He said to him, "So shall your descendants be." And he believed in the Lord, and He accounted it to him for righteousness." (**Genesis 15:1-6**)

When the Bible said Abraham believed God and it was accounted to him for righteousness, what the Bible meant was that because of God's covenant with him, Abraham has obtained the very righteousness of God.

"Abraham believed God, and it was accounted to him for Righteousness" **(Genesis 15:6).**

He became righteousness in the same way God is righteousness. The intimacy or the coming together in the covenant made Abraham what God is. God is righteousness. God crediting Righteousness to you means calling you what He is. I'm putting on you the virtue that is me. Even as believers today, we are the righteousness of God in Christ.

"For He made Him who knew no sin to be sin for us, that we might become the righteousness of God in Him." (**2 Corinthians 5:21**)

I see some people thinking, can you say categorically that you are righteousness? Why can you say you are righteousness? The Bible says that is who you are. You are that because you have entered a covenant with God.

So what Abraham is, you are. Righteousness on two legs. You are the righteousness not of man, but of God. Do you get it?

This means that you are in a personal relationship with God. If you know yourself as righteousness, no matter where you find yourself, the way you act, the way you compose, the things you say, how you behave will mirror the righteousness of God.

CHAPTER THIRTEEN

EMPOWERED BY THE COVENANT

"I will sing of the mercies of the Lord forever; With my mouth will I make known Your faithfulness to all generations. For I have said, "Mercy shall be built up forever; Your faithfulness You shall establish in the very heavens." "I have made a covenant with My chosen, I have sworn to My servant David: 'Your seed I will establish forever and build up your throne to all generations.'" Selah" (**Psalm 89:1-4**)

I used this text to introduce this chapter and my conversation with the Lord and to go beyond the text and get to the reasoning behind the thought process of God and this will be a blessing to us.

Verses 3 and 4 says, *"I have made a covenant with My chosen, I have sworn to My servant David: 'Your seed I will establish forever and build up your throne to all generations.'"*

Why did God make this covenant? What was the purpose of this covenant? What exactly is God looking for when He says: "I am making a covenant..."? If we chose to personalize these questions, they would come in this format: Why did God make covenants? What was the purpose of covenants?

To understand these questions and get to the heart of the Lord with regards to covenants, we must examine the God-established covenants in the Bible and draw from it the heart of God Himself. We highlight the scriptures that relate to the 5 main covenants

God made with man and then, make comments on these, starting with the Noahic Covenant.

- ***Noahic***

"And God said to Noah, "The end of all flesh has come before Me, for the earth is filled with violence through them; and behold, I will destroy them with the earth...And behold, I Myself am bringing floodwaters on the earth, to destroy from under heaven all flesh in which is the breath of life; everything that is on the earth shall die. But I will establish My covenant with you; and you shall go into the ark—you, your sons, your wife, and your sons' wives with you."" (**Genesis 6:13,17-18**)

- ***Abrahamic***

"Now the Lord had said to Abram: "Get out of your country, from your family and from your father's house to a land that I will show you. I will make you a great nation; I will bless you and make your name great; and you shall be a blessing. I will bless those who bless you, and I will curse him who curses you; and in you all the families of the earth shall be blessed."" (**Genesis 12:1-3**)

"When Abram was ninety-nine years old, the Lord appeared to Abram and said to him, "I am Almighty God; walk before Me and be blameless. And I will make My covenant between Me and you and will multiply you exceedingly."" (**Genesis 17:1-2**)

- ***Mosaic***

"And Moses went up to God, and the Lord called to him from the mountain, saying, "Thus you shall say to the house of Jacob, and tell the children of Israel: 'You have seen what I did to the Egyptians, and how I bore you on eagles' wings and brought you to Myself. Now therefore, if you will indeed obey My voice and keep My covenant, then you shall be a special treasure to Me above all people; for all the earth is Mine. And you shall be to Me a kingdom of priests and a holy

nation.' These are the words which you shall speak to the children of Israel."' (**Exodus 19:3-6**)

- ***Davidic***

For I have said, "Mercy shall be built up forever; Your faithfulness You shall establish in the very heavens." "I have made a covenant with My chosen, I have sworn to My servant David: 'Your seed I will establish forever and build up your throne to all generations.'" Selah" (**Psalm 89:2-4**)

- **New**

"But you are a chosen generation, a royal priesthood, a holy nation, His own special people, that you may proclaim the praises of Him who called you out of darkness into His marvelous light, who once were not a people but are now the people of God, who had not obtained mercy but now have obtained mercy." (**1 Peter 2:9-10**)

"Therefore, remember that you, once Gentiles in the flesh—who are called Uncircumcision by what is called the Circumcision made in the flesh by hands— that at that time you were without Christ, being aliens from the commonwealth of Israel and strangers from the covenants of promise, having no hope and without God in the world. But now in Christ Jesus you who once were far off have been brought near by the blood of Christ... Now, therefore, you are no longer strangers and foreigners, but fellow citizens with the saints and members of the household of God" (**Ephesians 2:11-13,19**)

- In the Noahic covenant, God got rid of all other people on earth and gave Noah a covenant.
- As for Abraham, he was asked to leave all his people and separate himself and then, was given a covenant.
- As for Moses, God said He wanted a people that would be a special treasure to Him.

- As for David, a unique King that would rule forever.
- And the new covenant talks about us being chosen when we were not a people of God but now a people of God.

For Abraham, has it ever been because of the land that was given? Was Moses leading the people in the land flowing with milk and honey just about the land? Is the promise to David that he will never lack a seed on the throne of Israel about the physical throne?

No, it means much more to God than the land, real estate, and the throne. It is about a deep intimate relationship with a people.

As we examine the pattern of God's covenants in the Bible, we see that there is a common theme of separation running across the various covenants. For example, in the Noahic covenant, God separated Noah and his family from the rest of the world by destroying it with a flood. In the Abrahamic covenant, God told Abraham to leave his idol-worshiping community and go to the land that God would show him. In the Mosaic covenant, God separated the Israelites from their life in slavery in Egypt by delivering them and bringing them to the wilderness.

This separation is necessary for God to make a covenant with his people. Many believers may claim the blessings and promises of their covenant with God, but it is important to understand the root of the covenant and the mind of God when he made it. In order to be a part of God's covenant, we must be a separated people, set apart from the world and its influences.

When we are called by God, we are not meant to be part of the world, but rather to be set apart from it. This is reflected in Jesus' prayer in John 17, where he asks that all His disciples be protected from the evil in the world and be kept from being like the rest of the world.

"I pray for them. I do not pray for the world but for those whom You have given Me, for they are Yours.... I do not pray that You should take them out of the world, but that You should keep them from the evil one. They are not of the world, just as I am not of the world." ***(John 17:9; 15-16)***

As I meditated on this, the Lord showed me that His covenant requires a separation of his people from the rest of the world. In order to be a part of God's covenant, we must not be like the rest of the world in our behavior, actions, words, or appearance, but rather be set apart for God. You can't be like them and be in God's covenant.

The instruction to be separate is an empowering instruction. In the new covenant, for example, I believe that you can be righteous because you have been empowered by the Lord to live a righteous life. No matter how much an unbeliever desires to live a righteous life, it would be like filthy rags before the Lord because it is not empowered by His Spirit.

Beloved, know that you have been empowered to live out the terms of your covenant with God. I will highlight five areas where we have been empowered.

1. ***The Covenant of God empowers you to be separate from the world.***

In all the covenants that God has cut, perhaps, except for the Davidic covenant, it is all about separating a people from the world; from the worldly system; about "walk before Me and be blameless" etc. In the writing of Paul to the church in Corinth, he said:

"And what agreement has the temple of God with idols? For you are the temple of the living God. As God has said: "I will dwell in them and walk among them. I will be their God, and they shall be My

people." Therefore, "Come out from among them and be separate, says the Lord. Do not touch what is unclean, and I will receive you." "I will be a Father to you, and you shall be My sons and daughters, says the Lord Almighty." (**2 Corinthians 6:16-18**)

When we get to the heart of the Father as to why He kept establishing covenants, we will conclude that He wants people who are separate...totally separate from the world. People live totally based on His covenant and the blessing and promises contained.

2. ***The Covenant of God empowers you to live for God and all that is God.***

It is not only what we have been separated from but who we are separated to. The covenant of God separates us to Himself. He wants to be our FATHER... and we His SONS AND DAUGHTERS.

God desires intimacy, closeness, a deep fellowship, etc., with His separated ones. Therefore, by covenant, He is committed, and by covenant, you are committed to the relationship.

"I do not pray for these alone, but also for those who will believe in Me through their word; that they all may be one, as You, Father, are in Me, and I in You; that they also may be one in Us, that the world may believe that You sent Me. And the glory which You gave Me I have given them, that they may be one just as We are one: I in them, and You in Me; that they may be made perfect in one, and that the world may know that You have sent Me, and have loved them as You have loved Me." (**John 17:20-23**)

Jesus, the mediator of the New Covenant prayed this over us – that we might be one with the Father and with the Son.

3. ***The Covenant of God empowers you to be committed to the rules that govern the kingdom of God.***

There are worldly rules, demonic rules, and even carnal rules... and all these rules compete for your attention and obedience. However, there are rules that govern the kingdom of God... and by covenant, you are empowered to walk and live by those rules.

"For you were once darkness, but now you are light in the Lord. Walk as children of light" (**Ephesians 5:8**)

Rules that govern holy living; that governs tithing; that governs generosity; that governs forgiveness and mercy; that governs fellowship among brethren, etc... these are Kingdom of God rules that you and I are empowered to live by – by covenant.

4. ***The Covenant of God empowers you to walk and manifest the blessing.***

When God spoke covenant to Noah, He also spoke the blessing in Genesis 9; when He spoke covenant to Abraham, He also spoke the blessing in Genesis 12 and Genesis 17; when He spoke covenant to Moses, He also spoke the blessing in Deuteronomy 28; when He spoke covenant to us in the New Covenant, He also spoke the blessing in Ephesians 1

Beloved, to be empowered by covenant is to be empowered to walk and live out all the blessing of the Lord.

"Blessed be the God and Father of our Lord Jesus Christ, who has blessed us with every spiritual blessing in the heavenly places in Christ" (**Ephesians 1:3**)

"Grace and peace be multiplied to you in the knowledge of God and of Jesus our Lord, as His divine power has given to us all things that pertain to life and godliness, through the knowledge of Him who called us by glory and virtue, by which have been given to us exceedingly great and precious promises, that through these you may be partakers of the divine nature, having escaped the corruption that is in the world through lust." (**2 Peter 1:2-4**)

5. ***The Covenant of God empowers you to fulfil God's mission on earth.***

All those that God spoke covenant to (Noah, Abraham, Moses, David, Us), He requires them to walk with Him in the fulfillment of His purposes on earth.

- For Noah, it is to procreate and model a righteous life before a fresh generation.
- For Abraham, it is to separate Abraham and create a people unto Himself – a model nation among nations.
- For Moses, it is to establish the laws, statutes, and rule of God in a nation and make them walk with God – establishing consequences to actions.
- For David, it is to model righteousness...and raise his children to sit on the throne.
- For us, it is to build His church with Him, make disciples, and destroy the works of the devil.

Each one of us should be on God's mission on earth as part of His covenanted children. We run after whatever matters to Him; We engage in whatever He asks us to engage in; We do whatever He has commanded that we do; We passionately desire whatever He desires.

Right now, for covenanted children living under the new covenant, instructions are in Mark 16:15-18; Matthew 28:28-30; Acts 1:8, etc.

Apostle Paul modeled this in his statement:

"I have been crucified with Christ; it is no longer I who live, but Christ lives in me; and the life which I now live in the flesh I live by faith in

the Son of God, who loved me and gave Himself for me." (**Galatians 2:20**)

Those with a gentile mindset will read this scripture and not see the covenant ties contained within. For those with a covenant mindset, they will know that Paul is saying, by covenant in Christ, I am dead and the present life I live, I live by faith in the Son of God – who brought me into the new covenant.

CHAPTER FOURTEEN

COVENANT CASE STUDY (JONATHAN AND DAVID)

"And Saul said to him, "Whose son are you, young man?" So, David answered, "I am the son of your servant Jesse the Bethlehemite." Now when he had finished speaking to Saul, the soul of Jonathan was knit to the soul of David, and Jonathan loved him as his own soul. Saul took him that day and would not let him go home to his father's house anymore. Then Jonathan and David made a covenant because he loved him as his own soul. And Jonathan took off the robe that was on him and gave it to David, with his armor, even to his sword and his bow and his belt." (**1 Samuel 17:58-18:4**)

As we come to the latter chapters of this book, we pick up lessons from significant covenants between peoples and nations to home in many of the revelations contained in this book. As for covenant between nations, next chapter, we will explore the covenant between the nation of Israel and the Gibeonites. However, in this chapter, we will explore the covenant between two people – Jonathan and David.

These are two young men who understood what covenant meant. In the age in which they live, covenant was a normal thing that people understood. And as these two young men looked at each other, Jonathan may have said: "I am making a covenant with you David" and David must have said: "Amen, I agree and make a covenant with you Jonathan" and with both in agreement for a covenant, the covenant was established.

There are details in these verses and other references to David's covenant with Jonathan that we will explore and pick up lessons for ourselves as we embrace the covenant that God has with us and for us.

Love

The basis of God's covenant with mankind is His love and mercy. Here we see emphasis placed on Jonathan's love for David which formed the basis of their covenant. Twice, Jonathan's love for David was mentioned in as many verses.

"... the soul of Jonathan was knit to the soul of David, and Jonathan loved him as his own soul." (**1 Samuel 18:1**)

"Then Jonathan and David made a covenant, because he loved him as his own soul." (**1 Samuel 18:3**)

The amplified version of the Bible used the word "bonded" to explain that Jonathan's soul was knit to the soul of David which means that Jonathan sees David's soul as his soul. They have become tightly knit together in their souls. Why? Love.

Jonathan loved David as himself or as his own soul. And Saul took David that day and did not let him return to his father's house. There Jonathan made a covenant or cut a covenant with David because he loved David as himself.

The interpretation of that statement that "he loved him as himself" is that Jonathan swore to David that from this day, you become my blood brother. David is now a blood brother to Jonathan. And Jonathan is now a blood brother to David. Now, the covenant is even stronger than being natural siblings because it is an agreement that heaven backs up.

Now, the motivation for them to make a covenant with each other was love. The Bible said Jonathan loved David as his own soul. It was mentioned twice that Jonathan loved David. Why do you think that God made a covenant with you? Or with Abraham who is your father? It is because of love. Why did God send His only begotten son for you and me? It is because of love.

John 3:16 confirms this, it says *"For God so loved the world that He gave His only begotten Son, that whoever believes in Him should not perish but have everlasting life."*

So, you realize there that love was a motivation for the covenant between David and Jonathan. And love was also the same motivation for our covenant with God. That was why the Bible says in Romans 8, "who can separate us from the love of Christ," nothing can. Nothing can nullify the covenant that God has over your life unless you refuse the covenant.

The factor of separation from the love of Christ is not based on what Christ will do because he will always love you, but on your part, you can accept His love or move away. So, the covenant tells me that God loves you so much. Whatever desires you have, and whatever things are necessary for your life, love will provide it. Whatever is necessary for God's covenant to manifest in your life, the unfailing love of God will drive that unless you refuse the covenant of God.

It's important you know, as we've discussed previously, in other chapters, that covenant means, whatever is mine is yours, and whatever is yours is mine. Now, God says I love you and nothing can separate my love from you. Then He is automatically saying that whatever is mine is yours, and you can have access to them because I love you, because you're in covenant, because love is working.

When you see a man and a woman, especially when they just met and they just fall in love and the rest, they can give anything to each other. Hence the reason God will give you anything that pertains to life and godliness because He loves you. This scripture encourages me at all times: *"What then shall we say to these things? If God is for us, who can be against us? He who did not spare His own Son, but delivered Him up for us all, how shall He not with Him also freely give us all things?"* (**Romans 8:31-32**)

If God did not spare His own Son in giving Him to you because of love but delivered Him up, how shall He not with Him also freely give you all things?

I desire that by the time you are through with this book, you remember that you are a covenant child and God loves you.

The Exchanges

As Jonathan and David went into a covenant, there were two pieces of items that were exchanged between them. The first was an exchange of robes. The Bible said in there, Jonathan took off the robe that was on him and gave it to David. It was a symbol. What Jonathan was wearing was a royal robe. He was a crown prince. He was a king-to-be, and he was the one to take the throne after Saul. He was wearing that Kingly robe; the royal robe; the robe that the prince wore and then he took the robe off because he entered a covenant and put the robe on David.

The symbolism of that is this, what makes me Jonathan a Crown Prince, I have given to you, you are now David Jonathan, the Crown Prince. I am now Jonathan David, the shepherd boy. I need you to get this because this is how covenant works. When David put the rope on, he became the crown prince and it was confirmed in the spirit realm.

The throne was Jonathan's inheritance, but because of the covenant, he gave it to David. He said, my covenant brother, I become naked for you. I lose everything for you.

Now, when God decided that he was going to bring you into a covenant, he stripped his only son naked on the cross, so that we may put on His righteousness. *"For He made Him who knew no sin to be sin for us, that we might become the righteousness of God in Him."* (2 Cor 5:21) So by covenant, we put on Christ, and therefore wherever we go, we are Christ's Ambassador, and representative, we carry Christ wherever we go. Even Jonathan understood the principle of what he was doing when he gave the robe to David. He knew that David would be king now. This is confirmed through Jonathan's statement in 1 Samuel 23:

"And David stayed in strongholds in the wilderness and remained in the mountains in the Wilderness of Ziph. Saul sought him every day, but God did not deliver him into his hand. So, David saw that Saul had come out to seek his life. And David was in the Wilderness of Ziph in a forest. Then Jonathan, Saul's son, arose and went to David in the woods and strengthened his hand in God. And he said to him, "Do not fear, for the hand of Saul my father shall not find you. You shall be king over Israel, and I shall be next to you. Even my father Saul knows that." (**1 Samuel 23:14-18**)

Now, I want you to get this because as the Crown Prince, he is the one that's supposed to be next after his father, but because he has entered a covenant and has given the robe to David, he said, you David, you will be king and I'll just be next to you. So two of them made a covenant before the Lord. Now Saul was looking for David all over the place, even though Jonathan knew where David was, he could not tell his father because of the covenant love. He cannot break the terms of the covenant and tell his father because for him to hunt David is to break the terms of the covenant.

Through Christ, you have been brought into covenant with God, and the robe of righteousness that was on Jesus is not placed on you and if we extrapolate that, we see that on earth, we rule with the authority of Jesus and Jesus will be next to us – not in terms of weakness but in terms of an Encourager, an Advocate, etc. The commands Jesus gave that we heal the sick, raise the dead, cleanse the leper, make the lame walk, etc. is based on His authority conferred on us. He did not say we should pray to Him to do it but we do the healing, the deliverance, etc. All He promised us is that He will be next to us by saying: I will never leave you nor forsake you.

I'll be on your side, I will support you, I will be your shield, I'll be a succor, I will be a rock, but I won't do it for you. You will rule by covenant.

Galatians chapter three that we know about covenant says, for as many of you as were baptized into Christ have put on Christ. Jesus said in Matthew 28:18-19a, *"All authority has been given to Me in heaven and on earth. Go therefore..."* which means all power in heaven and on earth has been given to me (Jesus) but I delegate it to you, and he said, Go therefore, I released that power that was mine. I give it to you, go and do what you can do with it. This tells us the power of the Covenant, as we see in the time of David.

The second item that we did see that got exchanged was their armor. In verse four of first Samuel chapter 18, the Bible says, *"And Jonathan took off the robe that was on him and gave it to David, with his armor, even to his sword and his bow and his belt."*

Jonathan stripped himself of what will be protecting him. In those days, you had your sword, but you would also have a belt, the belt is to hold the sword and other battle materials in place.

Do you remember that before this, Saul tried to give David his armor when he was going to kill Goliath (1 Samuel 17), but David said I have not tried this? I've not tested it. I can't take it. I can't go and kill Goliath with this. What is the difference between Saul's and Jonathan's armor? The difference is that Jonathan's armor had a covenant in it. Saul's armor was temporary while Jonathan's armor was permanent, Jonathan gave him permanently.

Saul's armor was something that had no significance to David, but Jonathan's armor has significance. So when Jonathan was giving him his armor, it wasn't about whether it fit the size of David or not. It was a symbol of the covenant. What it means is that my life I will use to protect you. With all that is in me, I will protect you. And David equally will have that kind of mindset as well to say, with everything that I have, I will protect you. That was the exchange of the armor.

If you read further down 1 Samuel chapter 20. In my paraphrase, you see the story there where David knew without a shadow of a doubt that he was but a little distance from death. Because Saul had determined to kill him. And Jonathan said, No, my father will not do that. He doesn't want to kill you. David said, No, he wants to. And then they made a covenant again. And Jonathan said, I will go and sit in the king's palace and the king's table and your seat will be empty. I will sit and see what my father says. When David was not at the seat the first day, Saul said nothing. Saul was thinking, He is a bad man anyway, maybe something bad has happened to him, and that's why he's not in the king's seat.

On the second day, David was not in his seat. And then Saul asked Jonathan and said, where is David? And Jonathan said in my paraphrase, 'oh, David took an excuse from me. He said they are doing something today is his Father's house and I grant him permission to go for that'. And then Saul just went ballistic, he said, you son of a harlot. Have you not sworn to David to your mother's nakedness? and just said some horrible things to Jonathan. And when Jonathan asked, what did David do to you, he took a spear and really wanted to kill his son on the basis of David. And he said, today that David must die, Jonathan knew for real, that his father really wants to kill David. And Jonathan went to tell David and said, David, now you can go, I know my father wants to kill you.

Now, if there were no covenants, David literally was a threat to the throne of Jonathan. Jonathan may not have known that Samuel secretly went to the house of Jesse to anoint David to be the next King, and he might not have known that David had been anointed king by the prophet. And even if he had known, David was a threat to his throne. But when covenant was in operation, rather than see David as a competitor, he saw David as one to promote, he saw David as one to protect, he saw David as one to lift, he saw David as one to encourage, and he saw David as a one that will support over his father.

Fast forward time. Saul died. Jonathan died. And the house of Saul became weak and virtually, nonexistent. David occupied the palace. The same word Jonathan said, you will be king. I've given you the robe. David had become king, and the covenant was still speaking.

Benefitting from the Covenant

"Now David said, "Is there still anyone who is left of the house of Saul, that I may show him kindness for Jonathan's sake?" And there was a servant of the house of Saul whose name was Ziba. So, when they had called him to David, the king said to him, "Are you Ziba?" He said, "At your service!" Then the king said, "Is there not still someone of the house of Saul, to whom I may show the kindness of God?" And Ziba said to the king, "There is still a son of Jonathan who is lame in his feet." So, the king said to him, "Where is he?" And Ziba said to the king, "Indeed he is in the house of Machir the son of Ammiel, in Lo Debar." Then King David sent and brought him out of the house of Machir the son of Ammiel, from Lo Debar.

Now when Mephibosheth the son of Jonathan, the son of Saul, had come to David, he fell on his face and prostrated himself. Then David said, "Mephibosheth?" And he answered, "Here is your servant!" So David said to him, "Do not fear, for I will surely show you kindness for Jonathan your father's sake, and will restore to you all the land of Saul your grandfather; and you shall eat bread at my table continually." Then he bowed himself, and said, "What is your servant, that you should look upon such a dead dog as I?"

And the king called to Ziba, Saul's servant, and said to him, "I have given to your master's son all that belonged to Saul and to all his house. You therefore, and your sons and your servants, shall work the land for him, and you shall bring in the harvest, that your master's son may have food to eat. But Mephibosheth your master's son shall eat bread at my table always." Now Ziba had fifteen sons and twenty servants. Then Ziba said to the king, "According to all that my lord the king has commanded his servant, so will your servant do."

*"As for Mephibosheth," said the king, "he shall eat at my table like one of the king's sons." Mephibosheth had a young son whose name was Micha. And all who dwelt in the house of Ziba were servants of Mephibosheth." (**2 Samuel 9:1-12**)*

David knew he was covenanted to Jonathan and based on the nature of covenant, it is not just an individual to an individual as in this case, but the covenant goes into generations and generations benefitting from the covenant enacted.

David declared and said, *"Is there still anyone who is left of the house of Saul, that I may show him kindness for Jonathan's sake?" the CEV version of the Bible puts it better: "One day, David thought, "I wonder if any of Saul's family are still alive. If they are, I will be kind to them, because I made a promise to Jonathan."* The point David was referring to here is that he wanted to express covenant love or mercy to a descendant of Saul (preferably Jonathan) because of the covenant that is in place.

The only child of Jonathan, Mephibosheth didn't even know his father was in covenant. He didn't even know that the covenant existed. He didn't know that there was a covenant that he could lay hold of. If he knew, he could have knocked on the doors of David a long time ago, and David would have had no choice but to execute covenant kindness, but he did not know. But David remembered his covenant one day and said, there must be somebody left, there must be somebody. There's an inheritance for somebody.

Irrespective of the fact that Mephibosheth was lame on both feet; he was perhaps, uneducated, poor, and uncultured. Irrespective of the fact that it is publicly known that the family of Saul and that of David were not on good terms and that, Mephibosheth had dwelt within a poor and humble setting, his father's (Jonathan's) covenant with David will trump all these inadequacies.

On that day that the covenant was remembered and put into action, Mephibosheth became one of the king's sons overnight. All that was lost from his father and grandfather were restored. Again, Mephibosheth can live in the palace as would have happened had Jonathan succeeded Saul as king.

I do list some of the other benefits to Mephibosheth once this covenant blessing was released upon him:

1. There is the restoration of lost possessions and inheritance.
2. The covenant blessing made him sit and dine with the king. Taking this a step further, he would have dined with kings, rulers, and those in power.
3. The covenant blessing gave him servants and servants of servants who were producing for him. With the number of Ziba's children and servants, Mephibosheth was already in charge of a lot of employees.

4. The covenant blessing brought him into purpose and destiny.

5. The covenant blessing guarantees the generation of Mephibosheth beyond him.

Imagine how much time Mephibosheth potentially lost because he did not know of this covenant and his entitlement to the covenant blessing.

We all have an inheritance in Christ, the promise of Abraham inherited in Christ, but many don't know this. You need to remember you are a covenant child. When God promised Abraham, He promised you as well.

CHAPTER FIFTEEN

COVENANT CASE STUDY (ISRAEL AND GIBEON)

"You shall make no covenant with them, nor with their gods." (**Exodus 23:32**)

As we enter the last chapter of this book, we look at the story of Israel and the Gibeonites. These are two separate nations and the Bible passages that we will study for this chapter will be in Joshua 9 and Joshua 10:1-15.

We will highlight certain verses within these two chapters to home the point in this case study but I will advise that you read these two chapters of the Bible for better understanding.

Now, the story we have here is quite a cogent story. Quite an interesting story. We have this set of people, the Gibeonites, they are a large city. In fact, the Bible said they are like a royal city. But they knew what the children of Israel has done to Jericho and Ai, and how they had destroyed them. And they decided that they are going to devise a scheme. The scheme is this, we're going to wear old torn sandals, we're going to look for wineskins that are very old and patched up and put some wine in it, and we're going to take some bread that is moldy, and take it with us and deceive them, that we have come from a very far country, meanwhile, they were just next door. You know, and the whole idea is that if we can make these people make a covenant with us, we are safe.

For ease of reading and understanding, I will write in bullet point format to home what you should note about this case study and about covenant in general.

This was a covenant that was cut in deception.

*"So, they said to him: "From a very far country your servants have come, because of the name of the Lord your God; for we have heard of His fame, and all that He did in Egypt, and all that He did to the two kings of the Amorites who were beyond the Jordan—to Sihon king of Heshbon, and Og king of Bashan, who was at Ashtaroth. Therefore, our elders and all the inhabitants of our country spoke to us, saying, 'Take provisions with you for the journey, and go to meet them, and say to them, "We are your servants; now therefore, make a covenant with us."' This bread of ours we took hot for our provision from our houses on the day we departed to come to you. But now look, it is dry and moldy. And these wineskins which we filled were new, and see, they are torn; and these our garments and our sandals have become old because of the very long journey." Then the men of Israel took some of their provisions; but they did not ask counsel of the Lord. So, Joshua made peace with them, and made a covenant with them to let them live; and the rulers of the congregation swore to them." (**vv9-15**)*

*"And it happened at the end of three days, after they had made a covenant with them, that they heard that they were their neighbors who dwelt near them." (**v16**)*

"So, they answered Joshua and said, "Because your servants were clearly told that the Lord your God commanded His servant

Moses to give you all the land, and to destroy all the inhabitants of the land from before you; therefore, we were very much afraid for our lives because of you and have done this thing." (**v24**)

They were really part of the Hivites who had planned to attack Joshua and the rest of the children of Israel. However, this tribe of Gibeonites did not follow what the general Hivites decided to do instead, they thought of a way of entering into a covenant with these covenanted people.

Yes, the Lord has said to Israel that they should destroy everything on their path to the promised land and make no covenant with them. But the Gibeonites thought they can convince Israel to make a covenant with them, and based on the covenant, they cannot destroy us.

Then Joshua and the elders of Israel made a covenant with them, and swore in the name of the Lord, that they will ever protect these people. But after three days that they made this covenant, the story became clear. Guys, you are not from any far country. You are just next door. You have deceived us. And if it's you and I, you will try to say, you cheat, you deceive me, the covenant doesn't stand. You lied to me. So, what I have said, I'm not going to hold on to it. But they dare not, because they have made a covenant.

You see, a Gentile mindset will make you say, I'm not doing anymore because this person did this. But once you have opened your mouth and said something in the name of the Lord, you are bound by it.

Israel could not get out of the covenant because they fear the covenant-keeping God.

"But the children of Israel did not attack them, because the rulers of the congregation had sworn to them by the Lord God of Israel. And all the congregation complained against the rulers. Then all the rulers said to all the congregation, "We have sworn to them by the Lord God of Israel; now therefore, we may not touch them. This we will do to them: We will let them live, lest wrath be upon us because of the oath which we swore to them." And the rulers said to them, "Let them live, but let them be woodcutters and water carriers for all the congregation, as the rulers had promised them." (**vv18-21**)

Why would they fear that wrath will be upon them because they understood the nature of a covenant. When a covenant is cut, it lasts, and it endures.

"When you make a vow to God, do not delay to pay it; For He has no pleasure in fools. Pay what you have vowed—Better not to vow than to vow and not pay." (**Ecclesiastes 5:4-5**)

This should give us the context of the covenant we have with God that it cannot be broken or annulled. The elders of Israel said they said we can't break the covenant, lest the wrath of God come upon us. And they have to honor the covenant even though the covenant was made in deceit. I need us to get this: If the covenant that was made by deceit cannot be annulled, how much more the covenant that God intentionally made with you. If the covenant that came out of lies, cannot be annulled, and cannot be canceled, how much more the covenant that God said I make with you. It can never be canceled.

You become what your covenant partner says you are or what you are to have. This is mainly in terms of the senior covenant partner to the junior covenant partner.

"And now, here we are, in your hands; do with us as it seems good and right to do to us." So, he did to them, and delivered them out of the hand of the children of Israel, so that they did not kill them. And that day Joshua made them woodcutters and water carriers for the congregation and for the altar of the Lord, in the place which He would choose, even to this day." (**vv25-27**)

When the children of Israel decided that okay because we have made this covenant, we will not kill you. Instead, they said, you will become woodcutters and carriers of water for us and for the house of the Lord. At least they didn't die. You see the promise, the promise is that we will protect you, that's the key thing, and they are to protect them. The term of this covenant was protection and that, they will get from Israel.

Joshua and the children of Israel were not kind to these Gibeonites. They cursed them and made them woodcutters and water carriers perpetually. The Bible records that so it is even to this day.

However, our senior covenant partner – even Jehovah God – speaks better things for us. He speaks blessing; He speaks purpose; He speaks empowerment; He speaks eternal bliss etc.

We are who God says we are – by covenant.

When trouble came, the Gibeonites turned to their covenant partner for help.

"Therefore, the five kings of the Amorites, the king of Jerusalem, the king of Hebron, the king of Jarmuth, the king of Lachish, and

the king of Eglon, gathered together and went up, they and all their armies, and camped before Gibeon and made war against it. And the men of Gibeon sent to Joshua at the camp at Gilgal, saying, "Do not forsake your servants; come up to us quickly, save us and help us, for all the kings of the Amorites who dwell in the mountains have gathered together against us." So, Joshua ascended from Gilgal, he and all the people of war with him, and all the mighty men of valor." (**vv10:5-7**)

Now, a time came when these Gibeonites were attacked by Kings around them, and they had the audacity to cry out to Joshua because of the covenant. They did call Joshua and say, Joshua, your servants have been attacked.

It is amazing the audacity of these Gibeonites who got into covenant by deception, but covenant is covenant. They have a covenant and they called on their covenant partner... and the covenant partner knows that he has no choice but to show up.

The God that has protected you must come and protect us. They have their army, and the army was strong, but they knew that by their own army, they can't defeat these five kingdoms, these five kings. So, they said, we don't have a covenant with God directly, but we have a covenant with those that had covenant with God. So, the God that protects the covenanted ones will come and protect us because we have a covenant with the covenanted ones.

Joshua did not come up and say, you slimy people. You lied to me to get a covenant, now you're calling me to come and protect you, which you and I may have done in the natural saying I'm not a fool. But Joshua didn't have a choice. He had made a covenant. And because he had made a covenant, he had to go based on his covenant with the Gibeonites and protect those people. So, the children of Israel had to put their own life at risk for the people that got covenant by deception. If Joshua could not annul and say, I won't go and do it, based on the covenant, what makes you think that God would not arise on your behalf because of the covenant. Did you get it? If the covenant was made out of deceit, yet, Joshua could not but go and defend them? What makes you think that in any type of situation, you may be, God will not arise and defend you likewise, even much more? It's an assurance of what covenant is.

If the same covenant partner that cursed the Gibeonites can turn up when covenant demand is made, how much more will your God – the Covenant Keeping God – arise for you when you need help. Any help for that matter!

God backs up those that will keep His covenant and keep other covenants they have made.

*"And the Lord said to Joshua, "Do not fear them, for I have delivered them into your hand; not a man of them shall stand before you." Joshua therefore came upon them suddenly, having marched all night from Gilgal. So, the Lord routed them before Israel, killed them with a great slaughter at Gibeon, chased them along the road that goes to Beth Horon, and struck them down as far as Azekah and Makkedah. And it happened, as they fled before Israel and were on the descent of Beth Horon, that the Lord cast down large hailstones from heaven on them as far as Azekah, and they died. There were more who died from the hailstones than the children of Israel killed with the sword." (**vv8-11**)*

Joshua was committed to keeping his covenant with the Gibeonites regardless and God honored that. God said: *"Do not fear them, for I have delivered them into your hand; not a man of them shall stand before you."* And at the end, it recorded that: *"There were more who died from the hailstones than the children of Israel killed with the sword."*

Then Joshua and the children of Israel went to fight these people. God now is committed to defending the Gibeonites – not for the sake of the Gibeonites but because of His covenanted people Israel. Did God want to really defend the Gibeonites? maybe not, because it's part of the people they were supposed to destroy. God didn't have the plan to save the Gibeonites in the grand scheme of things. But because Joshua has entered a covenant with them, God is now committed. God had to come in, to fight for them. In fact, it is recorded, that the number of people that God killed with hailstones more people than the children of Israel killed with the sword.

Again, I come to tell you, if he will rain hailstones for some people, He is not in direct covenant relationship with but because of His covenanted children - Israel, will he not rise up in whatever it takes to defend you? If you will trust and depend on Him that He will do so.

God who is the covenant partner of Joshua has also become the covenant partner of the Gibeonites through Israel.

How well do you keep your marriage covenant – for example? It is a covenant with another person and God will relate with you on how you keep that covenant... for example:

*"Husbands, in the same way be considerate as you live with your wives and treat them with respect as the weaker partner and as heirs with you of the gracious gift of life, so that nothing will hinder your prayers." (**1 Peter 3:7**)*

If you honor the covenant with your covenant spouse, God will honor your prayers. If you break your covenant promise with your covenant spouse, for example, God sees you as a covenant breaker and thereby, not obliged to answer your prayers.

God plagued the children of Israel when they broke the Gibeon-Covenant.

Although this covenant was born out of deceit, yet God confirms it as long as it was a covenant. You just don't break God-honored covenant because you don't like it anymore or because you don't like the man or woman to whom you made the covenant... God will hold you responsible!

In another portion of scripture regarding the Gibeonites and for us to see how God honors covenant, Saul tries to appease the children of Israel because the children of Israel never liked the Giboenites. But there's nothing they can do because a covenant exists, and it is perpetual. Reading from the second book of Samuel, we see this story.

"Now there was a famine in the days of David for three years, year after year; and David inquired of the Lord. And the Lord answered, "It is because of Saul and his bloodthirsty house, because he killed the Gibeonites." So, the king called the Gibeonites and spoke to them. Now the Gibeonites were not of the children of Israel, but of the remnant of the Amorites; the children of Israel had sworn protection to them, but Saul had

sought to kill them in his zeal for the children of Israel and Judah. Therefore, David said to the Gibeonites, "What shall I do for you? And with what shall I make atonement, that you may bless the inheritance of the Lord?" And the Gibeonites said to him, "We will have no silver or gold from Saul or from his house, nor shall you kill any man in Israel for us." So, he said, "Whatever you say, I will do for you." Then they answered the king, "As for the man who consumed us and plotted against us, that we should be destroyed from remaining in any of the territories of Israel, let seven men of his descendants be delivered to us, and we will hang them before the Lord in Gibeah of Saul, whom the Lord chose." And the king said, "I will give them." (**2 Samuel 21:1-6**)

Saul came into the scene hundreds of years later after the covenant has been enacted. And he knew that it was by covenant that these people stayed in the land of Israel, but he chose to ignore that and afflicted them and killed them. And the Lord in heaven, the covenant-keeping God would not let you break your covenant and expect him to keep his own covenant. You can't break the covenant you have made with man and expect God to keep the covenant he made with you. Do you get it? You can't enter a covenant of marriage for example, and say you just rascally walk away from it, and expect that God in heaven will honor the covenant over your own life. No wonder the Bible was saying in the book of Peter that treat your wives as weaker as vessels, so that your prayer will not be hindered. Because once you break the covenant, I will not honor the covenant over your own life. Your prayer will be useless.

So, when Saul killed the Gibeonites, God made sure there was a famine in the land, three years in a row. First-year, David didn't get it. He thought it was weather conditions. It was climate change. It was the ozone layer or something. It was whatever. The second year there was no rain, and he was thinking it was a coincidence. Maybe there was something else. The third year, there was famine and David had to say, you know, it's time to seek the Lord. Why are we having famine year after year? David sought the Lord. Why am I in this situation? Why is this going on? And God said, it is because of that bloodthirsty Saul.

Now, David was more of a warrior than Saul was. David killed more people than Saul killed, but Saul killed covenanted people while David killed uncovenanted people. Saul killed these covenanted people and God took the repercussions. David knew that he couldn't go and fight the Gibeonites and say, oh, you got to bless us by force. No, David had to go appealing and say how can we make atonement. What can we do? That you may bless us. The same people who are the servants are the same ones that need to bless their master now because the master broke the covenant.

You know, sometimes you think that because you are powerful, you can do whatever you like. But you see God, the one that watches over everything, is a covenant-keeping God, and will not allow you to break a covenant, only for you to now go to him and say he should bless you. No, you would not. David had to go meet the guys and say, you know, what? What do you want us to do? Then the Gibeonites responded, we don't want money or gold from Saul's house. We don't want any of that. But give us seven of his descendants and we are going to hang them at the gates of the city so that the rest of the children of Israel will know you don't break covenant.

Why are we ending this book with this case study? It is for us all to know that we are in covenant with God and that God will never break his covenant. However, if the covenant is not working for you, you need to go and ask God. Why is it not working? If a covenant that was made out of deceit cannot be broken, even hundreds of years later, from the time of Joshua to the time of Saul, God was still holding them to the covenant, then God's covenant with you cannot be broken except you walk away from it. God is going to hold you to every covenant you have made: covenant in marriage; covenant in deals; covenant in whatever. He will want you to honor your covenant and he will honor his own. But you can be sure of one thing. If the covenant that was made out of deceit cannot be broken, then the covenant that he has made with you cannot be broken. Amen.

We will end by making the declaration confirming God as our covenant partner.

Declaration

Heavenly Father, Jehovah God, you are my covenant partner. I'm in covenant with you, through the blood of Jesus, and through the blood of Jesus, I am connected to the covenant promises of Abraham, Isaac, and Jacob. I am an heir and one that inherits all those promises. And right now, I invite you, my covenant partner, into my life, into my home, and do what you do. Manifest Your covenant promises in full in my life, in my home, in my family, from this day forward in the name of Jesus. I will always view you and know you, as a covenant-keeping God and as Father God, over my life, and my family, in the name of Jesus. Thank you, Heavenly Father, in Jesus' name.

Printed in Great Britain
by Amazon